STATISTICS FOR PUBLIC ADMINISTRATION

Practical Uses for Better Decision Making

Maureen Berner

Recent Titles from ICMA Press

Green Books—Authoritative source books on local government management

The Effective Local Government Manager, 3rd edition
Emergency Management: Principles and Practice for Local Government, 2nd edition
Local Government Police Management, 4th edition
Local Planning: Contemporary Principles and Practice
Management Policies in Local Government Finance, 5th edition
Managing Fire and Rescue Services

Other recent titles

Capital Budgeting and Finance: A Guide for Local Governments, 2nd edition
Citizen Surveys for Local Government: A Comprehensive Guide to Making Them Matter
Economic Development: Strategies for State and Local Practice, 2nd edition
Effective Supervisory Practices, 4th edition
Human Resource Management in Local Government, 3rd edition
Leading Your Community: A Guide for Local Elected Leaders
Managing Local Government: Cases in Effectiveness
Managing Local Government Services: A Practical Guide

BV-SFICOC-210043

SUSTAINABLE
FORESTRY
INITIATIVE

Certified Fiber Sourcing
www.sfiprogram.org

The cover is not SFI.
The text in this book is printed using paper that is SFI Certified Fiber Source.

STATISTICS FOR PUBLIC ADMINISTRATION

Practical Uses for Better Decision Making

Maureen Berner
School of Government
University of North Carolina at Chapel Hill

ICMA PRESS

Leaders at the Core of Better Communities

ICMA advances professional local government worldwide. Its mission is to create excellence in local governance by developing and advancing professional management of local government. ICMA, the International City/County Management Association, provides member support; publications, data, and information; peer and results-oriented assistance; and training and professional development to more than 9,000 city, town, and county experts and other individuals and organizations throughout the world. The management decisions made by ICMA's members affect 185 million individuals living in thousands of communities, from small villages and towns to large metropolitan areas.

Library of Congress Cataloging-in-Publication Data

Berner, Maureen.
  Statistics for public administration : practical uses for better decision making / Maureen Berner.
     p. cm.
  ISBN 978-0-87326-192-0 (soft cover : alk. paper)
  1. Public administration--Statistical methods. I. Title.
  JA71.7.B67 2010
  001.4'22024351--dc22

                              2010013251

978-0-87326-192-0

Design and layout: Charles Mountain

Printed in the United States of America
2016   2015   2014   2013   2012   2011   2010
5 4 3 2 1

About the Author

Maureen Berner first joined the University of North Carolina (UNC) School of Government in 1998, teaching program evaluation, statistics, and budgeting. Between 2003 and 2005, she directed efforts at the University of Northern Iowa to provide new outreach activities for local governments based on the UNC model. In 2005, she returned to teaching and writing for MPA students and public officials at the School of Government. She has been active in research and teaching in both academia and government, and her publications include numerous books, book chapters, and journal articles. After earning her master's degree in public policy from Georgetown University in 1991, she worked for four years with the Budget Issues Group at the U.S. General Accounting Office, including a rotation to the U.S. House of Representatives Budget Committee, while serving as a presidential management intern. Berner received her doctorate in public policy from the LBJ School of Public Affairs, University of Texas at Austin.

Contents

Preface

To be successful, public administrators need to be able to analyze and evaluate policies, and to understand analyses and evaluations done by others. This book is designed to provide local government officials with the tools necessary to design analyses; gather, analyze, and interpret information; present results; and make recommendations. It is a book on research design and basic applied statistics. However, its primary purpose is not to help public managers master statistical theory; rather, it's to demonstrate how statistics can help them do their jobs better. At the same time, a minimal understanding and appreciation of statistical theory is necessary to use data correctly. My overall goal is to make public administrators educated consumers of statistical information.

Statistics is a language. A secondary goal of this book is to make public administrators effective translators. That is, a public employee needs to be able to communicate information to the appropriate audience, be it a local government manager, the city council, the board of trustees, the board of commissioners, a department head, or the public. After reading this book, you should be able to

- Understand and describe general approaches to and problems with public sector research and data measurement
- Conduct basic statistical analyses of raw data
- Evaluate statistical research performed by others.

The book progresses through roughly four stages. First, I introduce what I mean by "research." What does it mean to "do" research? How do you recognize research that is well done as opposed to poor or weak research?

Next, I cover the basic use of numbers: how to analyze data using descriptive statistics. What do data look like? The reader will understand the importance of getting a feel for the data in order to assess their usefulness. What kind of data are used in statistical research? How can you determine what data are good and what are bad? How can data be manipulated? What are the most common ways to summarize and present data? What do the most common statistics tell us about our data? More importantly, what can our data tell us about our issue (can't forget about that!)? What can't our data tell us?

Third, I show how to use data to draw conclusions and test for relationships. For example, is one thing, such as marketing, related to something else, such as the use of a recycling program? How can probability be useful to managers? How can it be used to assess risk? How can managers tell when something unusual has occurred? How do you move from merely describing a situation to evaluating it? How can you test an idea and be confident of your conclusions?

Finally, I introduce the principles of regression analysis, the most common of the more sophisticated social science research tools. Regression helps us understand *how* things are related. Is the relationship strong or weak, major or minor? Can we actually say something is causing something else? How does regression work? Why is it so popular in program analysis? What are its weaknesses and strengths? How does one interpret research using regression? Is it a useful tool for managers?

Throughout this book, I use the story of Chuck Edwards, the manager of Council Top, Iowa, to illustrate how a manager can use statistics in working through common local government problems. His assistant, Nina, helps quite a bit. She uses basic software programs, such as a spreadsheet program like Microsoft Excel, to do most of her work. Most data analysis can be done with spreadsheet programs. Even basic regression can be done with some special add-ons to standard spreadsheet programs. More advanced work, particularly multivariate regression, should be done with a specialized statistical program. Common statistical packages include SPSS, Stata, and SAS. However, these packages are relatively expensive and very powerful, and they can be overwhelming to a casual user, so I do not recommend that a local government purchase them unless it has devoted and trained staff to work on them regularly as well as a substantial amount of statistical work to be done.

I hesitate to mention many additional resources since they change so often, and any list I provide now will be quickly outdated. However, several resources have stood the test of time and should still be available when you are reading this. First, at the expense of being self-promoting, if you wish to understand more about research methods in general, I suggest *Research Methods of Public Administrators* (2002), a book I coauthored with Elizabethann O'Sullivan and Gary Rassel. For more on the mathematical background of statistics, I suggest consulting *Applied Statistics for Public Administration*, 7th ed. (2008), by Kenneth J. Meier, Jeffrey L. Brudney, and John Bohte. The classic minitext on regression analysis, and the one I always use as a supplement to other texts, is *Applied Regression: An Introduction* (1980), by Michael S. Lewis-Beck. The U.S. Government Accountability Office (GAO) has a number of excellent and accessible publications that provide information on various research methods, quantitative and qualitative, that can be used in program evaluation. I know from experience that every sentence in every publication by GAO is checked and rechecked and checked again by multiple experts against multiple sources.

This book will not train you to use the software or do the actual mathematical calculations; I do not provide an electronic file with data set up in a sample spreadsheet. Nor will this book give you a specific roadmap on how to answer a specific question. No book will do that; that is not how actual life, or management, works. Theory is just theory, not reality. You need to gather real data that are important for a problem facing you. You will really learn how to use statistics only if you need to use them. My goal, again, is to allow local government officials to understand how statistics can help them in their jobs in a real way—to be educated consumers of information.

The town of Council Top is based very loosely on a combination of Traer, Iowa, and Council Bluffs, Iowa, where my husband and I grew up, respectively. I have tremendous respect for the people of Iowa, and I taught some of the smartest, hardest-working, and most ethical undergraduate public administration students at the University of Northern Iowa. I currently have the honor of teaching some of the smartest, hardest-working, and most ethical graduate public administration students at the University of North Carolina at Chapel Hill. I applaud my faculty colleagues here, who are uniformly devoted to providing the best professional public administration training, especially for local government, in the country.

I want to thank the School of Government for providing incredible support in every aspect of my work. I also want to thank ICMA, devoted to excellence in local government management, for publishing this book.

The character of Chuck Edwards is loosely based on my oldest brother, whom I love very much (and not to any greater or lesser extent than any of my other four older brothers or older sister!). Nina is a really smart, cool, and caring German student. Maria is a really smart, cool, and caring Brazilian student. Rex and Will really do love Legos. I want to thank my husband, Andy, and my kids, William, Yvette, Maxwell, and, not the least, Leo (who had the wonderful timing of being born in the course of my writing this book) for allowing me time to write around taking care of them, my most important and fun job.

You Have to Answer a Question: Now What Do You Do?

[RESEARCH DESIGN]

"Chuck, you're crazy. How are you going to convince the council that this is a good idea?"

Chuck Edwards eased back in his chair. He had been city manager of Council Top for only a year, after serving three years as assistant manager. When he was hired, he found that most past decisions had been made thoughtfully, with good intentions, by good people—but that there was often little or no information to help the process along. Decisions were driven by anecdotes, by complaints from anywhere from one to ten people, or by someone who proposed an idea with which someone else agreed and everyone else went along. With his new position as manager, Chuck knew that he wanted to use information in a better way: to actually have numbers to back up good proposals, counter proposals that didn't sound quite right, and help him to figure out the difference.

The problem was, he wasn't used to using research, and he didn't have the time or energy to take a research course at the Western Community College. In fact, he really didn't want to "do" research; he just wanted to have some of his staff work with solid information rather than guesses. Well, that is not completely true. He wanted to be able to understand the numbers himself and then explain them to his council in a way that did not make him look like an idiot.

His proposal was to hire a management analyst—someone who would help him increase the city's capacity to crunch numbers. He had just told Joan, the human resource (HR) manager, that he wanted to develop a new position description that he could propose to the council at the next meeting. She was skeptical that it was going to be worth her time.

"Joan, I know the council is against hiring anyone who doesn't do something traditional, like keep the books or clean the streets or save people from burning buildings. But the city is growing, the decisions are a lot more complicated than they have been before, and a lot more money is at stake. We need better information and someone who can understand it. And we need to understand it. I don't want to be swamped under a lot of numbers and gobbledygook that you need a PhD to decipher. And I need to be able to explain it to the council in a way that makes decisions easier."

"I still don't think the council will go for it." Joan looked at Chuck over her glasses.

"All I have to do is bring up the fiasco over the planning for the senior center and remind them of how, having made a bunch of assumptions about who would use it and how, we built it completely wrong and just had to spend $3 million to revamp it. That cost the last manager her job, and I don't want a repeat. A management analyst will be a good investment if we can use information to avoid bad decisions."

"Well, when you bring that up, you might get the votes. I'll get the position description ready before Monday night."

This book is for Chuck, Joan, the new management analyst, the council, and any other public sector official who wants to use information, primarily numbers, to make better decisions. It will not make you a statistician or card-carrying data nerd. The objective is to make you an educated consumer of statistical information. That is, you will be able to understand and use statistical information, recognize what is involved in research, and distinguish between good analyses and poor ones. When the next consultant delivers a report, you will be able to actually read some of the chapters rather than just flipping to the conclusion and trusting that the consultant did the analysis correctly.

Throughout the book, you will see certain words in bold. Although these are terms often used by statisticians, they represent pretty simple concepts. We will introduce the official term and then explain the concept so that you can untangle "stats-talk."

Developing a good research design

The book is organized to help you understand statistics. Statistics are made up of numbers. But numbers don't just fall out of the sky. Before you crunch any data, you have to know exactly what it is that you want to know! In other words, what information would be really helpful to make a decision? What numbers should you collect? How can you get this information? And how can you know if it is any good?

This chapter walks you through the major steps you need to take before you even see your first number. If you can read only one chapter in this book, this is it.

Together, these eight steps represent the **research design process:**

- Understand the issue (identify the background and context)
- Identify the problem (write a problem statement)
- Explain what you think is going on (what is your theory?)
- Identify *generally* what you need to know to test your theory (what is the general research question?)
- Identify *more specifically* what you need to know to test your theory (what hypothesis do you want to test?)
- Identify *exactly* what you need to know to test your theory (how do you operationalize your hypothesis?)
- Figure out how you are going to gather that information (choose your methodology)
- Decide if the data you gather are good enough to answer your questions, inform your decision, and help you solve your problem.

Walking through the research design process

Why do we place such importance on this preliminary planning work? Simple: garbage in, garbage out. If we do not plan out our questions well, it is easy to fall into the trap of gathering data that sit on a shelf or, in this electronic age, in a computer file to be unused and forgotten. Let's walk briefly through these eight steps.

What is the issue?

Often we jump into gathering numbers before understanding what the context is. The first step of the research process is to **understand the issue** involved. In Council Top, Iowa, the fictional town that provides the context for this book, the population had been growing as people moved in from the dying small towns. The manager faced multiple issues that a manager would not have faced twenty years ago— increasing demands for technology, health care, social services, transportation, and housing services, to name a few. In real-life situations, the context would include information not just about a population and the services it needs but also about a sensitive political situation, upcoming elections, budgetary constraints, new state or federal mandates, reforms in related areas such as mental health services or educational testing, zoning controversies, public-private partnership, ethics, etc.

What is the problem?

Have you heard of people who have a great solution and are looking for a problem? The second step in developing a good research design is writing a **problem statement.** It can be difficult to develop a single sentence that captures exactly why you need to make a change or reach a decision, but this step is vital. A problem statement clearly and specifically states a situation that is, well, a problem. For example,

- The number of bicycle accidents has been increasing dramatically over the past five years.
- Six months from the end of the fiscal year, the public safety budget is already in the red.
- Seniors are complaining that local government services are too hard to access, which could lead to underuse of services, poorer health care, and lower quality of life for elderly people.
- Local government streets flood on a regular basis, inconveniencing residents and causing the roads to deteriorate.
- Animal control has reported over ten cases of rabid raccoons in the area, more than in any previous year, endangering public health and causing panic among suburban parents and pet owners.

Why bother with this step? If you cannot clearly state what the problem is, you cannot focus your research in a way that gets directly to the heart of the matter. You wander in a wilderness of data, not sure what will be helpful and what won't. You gather any data available, hoping that somewhere in the numbers is the key information you need. You might try to solve multiple problems at once, or the wrong problem, or even assume that there is a problem where there really is not one.

What do we think is going on?

This third step allows you to outline your theory of how different things or events relate to each other. In statistical terms, this is referred to as **developing a model.** A model is just a diagram of how you think various actors or situations relate to each other. A model can be very simplistic or very complex. For example, a simple model might show the following:

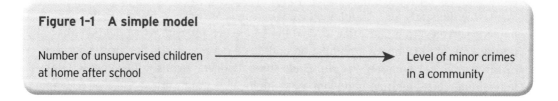

Figure 1-1   A simple model

Number of unsupervised children   ⟶   Level of minor crimes
at home after school   in a community

In this model, I am theorizing a particular relationship: that the number of unsupervised children at home after school is related to the level of minor crimes in a community. At this point, I am not sure this is the case; I have no evidence, or data, to support this theory. In fact, my model is not really complete. There are many other things that probably influence the level of minor crimes in a community. A more complete model might look like Figure 1–2:

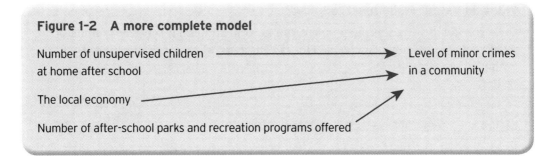

Figure 1-2   A more complete model

Number of unsupervised children at home after school ——————→ Level of minor crimes in a community

The local economy ——————→

Number of after-school parks and recreation programs offered

Just as there are simple relationships and complex ones, every model will be different depending on the situation we are trying to describe. Usually our task doesn't involve fully describing a model; we don't need to understand every connection. We are just interested in a few major relationships that we hope we can influence in our role as government officials.

What counts as a relationship? As we'll discuss in more detail in Chapter 8, a relationship needs four things:

- An appropriate **time order** between the things. In other words, what comes first?

- **Theoretical support.** Does the relationship make sense? Is it logical to think that greater numbers of unsupervised children might lead to greater numbers of minor crimes? Is it logical to think that if the local economy is poor, there will be a higher level of minor crimes?

- **Co-variation,** or the idea that the two parts of the relationship will move together, either both increasing or both decreasing (showing a **positive relationship,** such as more unsupervised children and more minor crime) or one increasing while the other decreases (showing a **negative,** or **inverse, relationship,** such as lower economic growth and higher crime).

- **Legitimacy.** Researchers are only measuring true relationships. In other words, they hope they are not measuring false, or **spurious,** relationships. For example, researchers have data showing that in months when Popsicle sales are higher, murder rates are also higher. So do Popsicles cause people to murder each other? To begin with, this relationship lacks theoretical support; that is, it fails the logic test. However, it also illustrates what researchers call a spurious relationship. There is not a true relationship between Popsicle consumption and murder rates. Instead, both are related to higher temperatures! In summer months, Popsicle consumption increases. Murder rates also tend to go up in summer months, perhaps because more people are outside and interacting with one another. But the two are not related—unless you're talking of the specific case when my older son eats the last Popsicle in front of my Popsicle-loving daughter.

What do we generally need to know?

Once you identify the specific problem you need to address, it is easier to think of what you need to know to solve it. This is your **general research question.** For example:

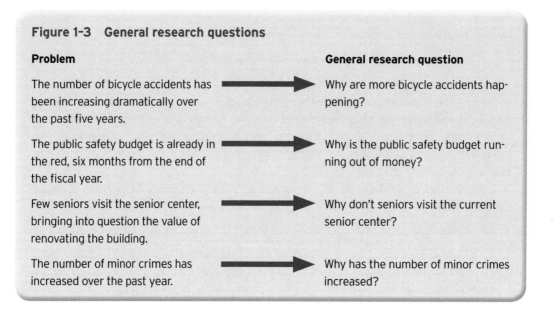

Figure 1-3   General research questions

Problem	General research question
The number of bicycle accidents has been increasing dramatically over the past five years.	Why are more bicycle accidents happening?
The public safety budget is already in the red, six months from the end of the fiscal year.	Why is the public safety budget running out of money?
Few seniors visit the senior center, bringing into question the value of renovating the building.	Why don't seniors visit the current senior center?
The number of minor crimes has increased over the past year.	Why has the number of minor crimes increased?

You will notice that each of the research questions can be answered with information. There is no subjectivity involved. We are not asking questions that begin with "Should the city do...?" or "What is the best way to...?" Those types of questions belong in the realm of opinion, judgment, experience, discussion, and debate. In this book, we are focused on using data to answer informational, evidenced-based questions.

What hypotheses do we want to test?

Next comes a step that most practitioners don't do—or at least they do it in their heads but don't usually put it down on paper. They create a **hypothesis** that they will test with data to help answer the research question. A hypothesis is really nothing more than stating your hunch or guess explicitly. If you create a hypothesis, it is easier to say "my guess was right" or "my guess was wrong"; this helps focus your research. Once you have your hypothesis laid out, you will gather data to see if it is true. In research terms, if we find support for our hypothesis, we will probably accept it. If we ask questions and do not find support for the hypothesis, we may reject it.

Look at Figure 1–4. Remember that the statements on the right are hypotheses, not statements of fact. We will be testing these statements. If we reject a hypothesis,

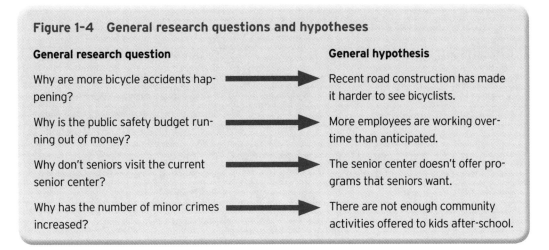

Figure 1-4   General research questions and hypotheses

General research question	General hypothesis
Why are more bicycle accidents happening?	Recent road construction has made it harder to see bicyclists.
Why is the public safety budget running out of money?	More employees are working overtime than anticipated.
Why don't seniors visit the current senior center?	The senior center doesn't offer programs that seniors want.
Why has the number of minor crimes increased?	There are not enough community activities offered to kids after-school.

we might form a new one. For example, if we don't find support for the hypothesis that the senior center doesn't offer programs that seniors want, we might think of a new hypothesis to test, such as that seniors don't visit the center because they cannot get to it easily. In the course of research, we might focus on testing one specific hypothesis because we have a certain explanation in mind, and once we confirm or reject it, our research is done. However, we might also be searching for an explanation more broadly. In that case, if we reject one hypothesis, we might turn our research to another hypothesis, and then another, and another until we find support. Or we might do some exploratory analysis to come up with other possible hypotheses; for example, we may conduct a survey with the seniors with open-ended questions about why they do or do not use the senior center. From their responses we can then form some more focused hypotheses to test.

What specific question would let us test the hypothesis, and how can we best phrase it?

At some point, we have to stop talking in generalities and be specific. That is, we have to ask a question we can actually answer, and we have to make sure that it is phrased so as to be most answerable. When we take something abstract—a hypothesis, for example—and put it into measurable terms, we **operationalize** it. In the statements shown in Figure 1–5 (see page 8), we move from our general hypothesis to something with which we can work. There are many ways a general hypothesis can be operationalized. The key is whether it can be tested and either supported or rejected. In research terms, we want the hypothesis to be **falsifiable.** We have to be able, at least theoretically, to disprove it. For example, I could hypothesize that life exists on other planets. However, I cannot disprove that hypothesis. I would have to show that no life exists on any other planet in the universe, and that is impossible

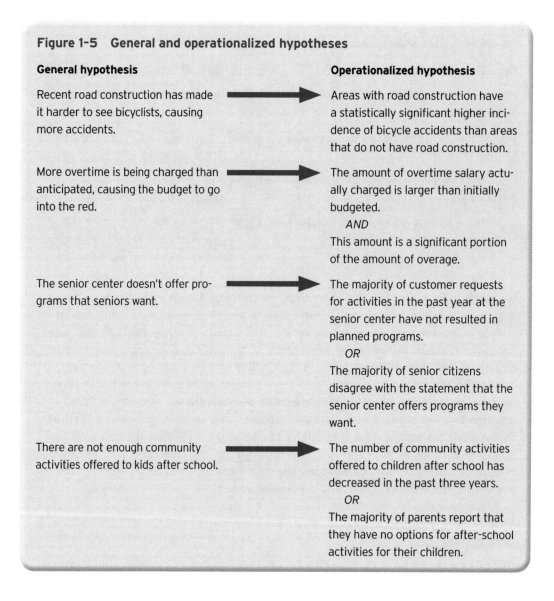

Figure 1-5   General and operationalized hypotheses

General hypothesis	Operationalized hypothesis
Recent road construction has made it harder to see bicyclists, causing more accidents.	Areas with road construction have a statistically significant higher incidence of bicycle accidents than areas that do not have road construction.
More overtime is being charged than anticipated, causing the budget to go into the red.	The amount of overtime salary actually charged is larger than initially budgeted. *AND* This amount is a significant portion of the amount of overage.
The senior center doesn't offer programs that seniors want.	The majority of customer requests for activities in the past year at the senior center have not resulted in planned programs. *OR* The majority of senior citizens disagree with the statement that the senior center offers programs they want.
There are not enough community activities offered to kids after school.	The number of community activities offered to children after school has decreased in the past three years. *OR* The majority of parents report that they have no options for after-school activities for their children.

(at least at this time). I would have to visit all the other planets and check for life. This cannot be a research hypothesis. Instead, I could form a research hypothesis that there is some form of life as we know it on Mars. Whether there is some form of life on Mars is something that we should be able to prove or disprove with current technology; in fact, scientists are trying to do just that.

We have now gone from a problem to a general research question to something we would actually be able measure and test. This is a positive thing! Probably one of the biggest mistakes in research is not spending enough time focusing the research question.

Public administrators are very familiar with the task of gathering data that turn out to be less useful than originally thought. An important point to consider now is whether the specific hypotheses you test will provide information that will be respected by decision makers. You can imagine having data to answer the specific, operationalized hypotheses such as the ones to the left. If you could confirm or reject these statements, would you be closer to a solution to your problem? If not, these hypotheses should be dropped and others formed. Don't spend time on gathering data that will not be used.

How are we going to gather data to test these hypotheses?

Some problems are so complex that they are very hard to understand, even with lots of studies and information and numbers. The continuing academic achievement gap between two different races is a wonderful example. It will likely take years, maybe decades, for researchers to understand why it persists. For the most important "why" questions, different sides may have conflicting data and statistics to back up their answers. Then the debate is not about the numbers but about the quality of the research design and data. There are two main ways that people assess the quality of research: by asking if the research design is solid and by asking if the data are good. First, let's discuss how we plan our work.

Research design　　Planning how to gather data is the **research design phase.** There are three main designs that can be used to conduct a research project: an experimental design, a quasi-experimental design, or a nonexperimental design. Most public administrators will never work with an experimental design, but it is helpful to understand what it is since it is the benchmark against which all other research is measured.

Experimental designs have two main characteristics. The first is **control,** as it applies to the setting, the participants, and the experiment setup. In fact, there is usually a **control group** to compare against the experimental group. Experimental designs are common in medical or laboratory studies. In a laboratory setting, for example, one set of mice may receive a new drug to prevent cancer while another set, the control group, may not. Researchers would then see if the mice in the experimental group develop fewer cases of cancer than those in the control group.

The second important characteristic is **random assignment.** Regarding how these two groups are formed, random assignment means that each person (or mouse, in this example) has an equal chance of being put in the experimental or control group. Why is this valuable? Because any differences between the groups will also be random. There is just as likely to be a fat mouse or a mouse genetically prone to cancer in one group as in the other group. There are no systematic differences between the groups, which means that there is no systematic bias between them. This does not mean that the groups are exactly alike. But there should not be *any pattern* to differences between them other than that due to the experimental drug.

Unfortunately, control is not something that public administrators have at their disposal. Experimental designs tend to be limited to laboratories, not community centers or housing offices or fire stations. If we are lucky, we might have a quasi-experimental design. **Quasi-experimental designs** are like they sound. They have one of the two aspects of an experimental design—a comparison group or random participation in the groups—but not both. For example, you might be able to start a mentorship program in one school and, after several years, compare student performance in that school to student performance in a school without a mentorship program. By comparing one school with the program to one without, we are using an experimental group and a control group, which meets one of the two criteria for an experimental design. But we can't meet the other criterion: we can't just randomly assign students from the community to the two schools. Therefore, there may be systematic differences between the student bodies in the schools—one may have a higher population of students from single-parent households, for example—that we need to take into account.

In a **nonexperimental design,** there is no control group, and participants are not randomly selected. An example of a nonexperimental design would be simply measuring the number of bicycle accidents both before a new safety program is implemented and after. Because we didn't control for other things that could have reduced bicycle accidents, such as colder weather, and we didn't select the groups of bikers at random, we don't know for certain if a reduction in accidents was due to our safety program or to something else.

Research quality   In terms of research quality, experimental designs are the strongest. This is why they are used so much in medical research. If you are considering prescribing a new treatment for cancer, you want to make sure that the treatment has been tested in the most rigorous way. To be honest, decisions about social problems are just as important, but since there is much less ability to control the situation, quasi-experimental designs are the next preferred approach, with nonexperimental designs coming in last. Unfortunately, city managers often have to rely on nonexperimental designs.

> The public and researchers alike will have stronger faith in the conclusions from a study if the study and its conclusions are replicable.

We assess quality of research in two ways: we ask if it is valid and we ask if it is reliable. These terms have meaning in our normal conversation and have similar, but more specific, meaning in research. For a research design to be **valid,** it has to answer the question we want it to answer. That may seem obvious and simplistic, but it is harder to achieve than you might think. If we want to know why seniors are not visiting the local senior center more often, it might be easiest to conduct a survey asking if they like the programs offered at the center. But the reasons that seniors may not be visiting the center may have nothing to do with the programming, so the questions wouldn't address the appropriate issue. Parking may be the issue. Or the survey may have been poorly distributed so that it did not reach the seniors who are likely to come to the center. If the study has major flaws in how it is carried out, it will not be considered valid.

For the study to be **reliable,** others would have to be able to replicate it and get similar results. This is the second test of a good study. The public and researchers alike will have stronger faith in the conclusions from a study if another person is able to conduct the same study.

As mentioned above, experimental designs are considered the strongest types of research. That is usually because the level of control we have and our ability to use random assignment to avoid bias mean that we can be more confident in the study's validity and reliability. But local government officials can't offer a housing program in a laboratory or randomly assign some people to receive food assistance and others to go hungry. Does that mean we shouldn't even try to use data to make decisions? Of course not. Even without a control group or random assignment, we may gather and use quality information.

How can we know if we have good data?

The qualities of validity and reliability apply to data, too. For validity, we ask if our data are really measuring what we want them to measure. Let's say you would like to understand how wealthy your community is. You might simply use Census Bureau information about average income in different neighborhoods as your data. For most purposes, average income will capture the differences in wealth across neighborhoods very well. But income does not measure assets such as land or stocks, so you would not really be capturing true wealth. On the other hand, financial aid officers at colleges understand how assets like land or a house may represent overall wealth, but since it is hard to sell a portion of a house or a few acres of farmland to help a child pay for college, these do not represent liquid assets. There are many measures of wealth, and it is important to understand exactly what measures you want to use to address the problem at hand.

> Good data measure what you are trying to measure.
> They accurately capture the concept.

Even with measures that you think are valid, you must be careful to make sure that the data are not skewed or mismeasured in some way. In which major at the University of North Carolina will you find graduates who make the highest salary on average? It is not pre-law or pre-med or business. Surprisingly, it is geography. That is because Michael Jordan, the star basketball player, was a geography major. Figures for average income are often skewed by very high or very low salaries. That is why we use median instead of average (mean) as a more valid measure of income. (More on averages, medians, and other descriptive statistics in the next chapter.) In the end, the concept of validity is best associated with the idea of accuracy. Are you measuring what you want to measure?

Reliability with regard to data is similar to reliability with regard to a research design. As discussed above, a reliable research design is one that can be replicated by others. In the same way, reliable data are those that are measured consistently so that if a different researcher makes the same measurement, he or she will obtain the same result. With data, the concept of reliability is best associated with precision.

To understand how reliability and validity work together, we can use the analogy of shooting at a target. Someone who shoots in a "valid" way will have all her shots hit the target near the bull's eye. Someone who shoots reliably will have all his shots hit the target in the same area, close together. Ideal data are both valid and reliable. That is, the shots will be both near the bull's eye and closely clustered.

"Chuck, the last candidate to interview is here," said Joan.

"Thank you, Joan," replied Chuck tiredly, looking up from the paltry pile of résumés on his desk. It couldn't really be called a stack. "I am just not sure people understand what we need. These candidates either don't like analysis, can't write or speak to explain the analysis, or think massive spreadsheets are the answer to everything."

"*I* am not sure what we need," said Joan with a smile. She ushered in a young woman in a business suit holding a faux-leather portfolio and wearing a nervous, friendly expression. She was a recent graduate from the MPA program at State. Joan introduced them. "This is Nina Schorn. Nina, Chuck Edwards, our manager."

After the usual pleasantries, Chuck got down to business. "I am looking for an analyst who can work with me and the staff in the manager's office. We need someone who can work with gathering, analyzing, and reporting information—data. Numbers. Maybe a lot of numbers. And we need someone who can explain the analysis to our staff and elected officials."

Chuck expected to see her flinch at this, as did the other two candidates he had interviewed. To his surprise, Nina visibly relaxed. "Well, I enjoy working with numbers. But I would rather not work with a lot of data."

"I don't understand," said Chuck, confused. "The position description clearly says the analyst must be able to work with statistics."

"I don't want to work with 'lots' of data; I want to work with the *right* data. If you ask the right questions, you only need a few answers to make better decisions," Nina said.

Chuck paused, looked down at her résumé, then looked up at her with a grin. "I think we will get on very well," said Chuck, pushing the rest of the résumés to the side of his desk.

Review questions

1. What would be examples of each of the following steps in the research design process?

   a. Understanding the issue

   b. Identifying the problem

   c. Explaining what you think is going on

   d. Identifying generally what you need to know to test your theory

   e. Identifying more specifically what you need to know to test your theory

   f. Identifying exactly what you need to know to test your theory

   g. Outlining how you are going to gather that information

   h. Determining that the data you gather will be good enough to answer your questions, inform your decisions, and help solve your problems.

2. Compose a problem statement that describes something going on in your jurisdiction.

3. Define and give examples of a positive relationship and a negative relationship.

4. Develop a general research question based on the problem statement from Question 2.

5. Develop a hypothesis from each of these general research questions about Council Top, Iowa:

   a. Why are test scores decreasing?

   b. Why has unemployment risen in the past five years?

   c. Why are energy costs rising?

   d. Why have crime rates fallen?

6. Take each hypothesis from Question 5 and describe how you could falsify it.

7. If you were going to conduct research on decreasing test scores, how would you go about using an experimental design?

8. Would an experiment with a control group that has not been randomly assigned be experimental, quasi-experimental, or nonexperimental? Why?

9. A scale in a doctor's office always adds five pounds to people being weighed. Is this scale valid? Is it reliable? Why or why not?

10. Can a researcher have a valid study but not have valid data? How about valid data but not a valid study?

Muck Around in the Numbers!

2

[DESCRIPTIVE STATISTICS]

Chuck stood at his desk at 6:40 p.m., printing off just one more document. The council meeting was starting in twenty minutes, and Chuck had a bad habit of waiting until the last minute before deciding he needed this document or that report handy just in case a council member asked a question he couldn't answer. Nina stopped by his door.

"Are you walking down?" she asked.

Chuck didn't want it to appear that he was scrambling at the last minute, so he ignored the appendixes to the planning report he was printing out. "Sure. Be right with you." *I don't really need those appendixes*, he thought. *No one is going to ask about average parking space sizes in Council Top.*

"Are you ready for your first report to the council?" asked Chuck.

"I think so. I wasn't able to gather all the data the council asked for, and I think it will be surprised why," said Nina, walking quickly. Chuck lengthened his stride to catch up. His staff was getting younger and faster, or he was getting older and slower. He preferred to think it was the former.

This chapter is about the basics of **data:** what data are. (And, by the way, the word *data* is always plural. A single piece of data is a datum; many pieces are data.) We start out by understanding the different kinds of data. You might ask, aren't data just numbers? No. Data are pieces of information, any kind of information. Some are numbers, some are not. Each piece of information is called an **observation.** If you are going to gather data—pieces of information—from fifteen people, you will gather fifteen observations. With more observations, you have more information. We will speak to this point again later, but just as it is always wise to have as much information as possible when making decisions, the same rule applies with statistics. In general, the more observations, the better. (At some point, more information can actually muddy the waters, but we will discuss that in more detail later as well.)

Remember that the goal of this entire process is to answer a question—the one that you identified in the previous chapter. We need information to answer that question. For example, your county commissioners may want to know if roads in the county are being kept free of trash. You can answer that question in a variety of ways. Typically, a county employee might respond by citing the amount of trash picked up over the previous six months, one measure that the roadways have been cleaned. But that doesn't mean that for every pound of trash picked up, another two weren't dropped. Another way to respond would be to cite the number of miles of roadway that have been "adopted" by community groups, or the number of groups—or the total membership of each (assuming that those groups are picking up the trash as expected!)—that has done the adopting. Yet another way would be to cite the number of county employee hours devoted to trash pickup or the amount of dollars allocated to contractors to clean roadways, although again, effort does not mean results. All these ways involve numbers, which is how we usually think of data. However, what if a county employee instead presented a video report highlighting the worst areas for littering and showing them both before and after county pickup efforts? Or a photo report prepared by citizens who were given free disposable cameras to photograph any major trash they encountered on their daily commutes? These observations are also data.

> Data are not just numbers; data are pieces of information.
> Names, colors, photos, and sounds can all be data.

Don't limit yourself to starting with numbers. Be creative. You should think about the best way to communicate your information, regardless of the form. But remember, too, that researchers are much more likely to use traditional forms of data in the work that you are likely to encounter.

Types of data

There are three main types of traditional data: nominal, ordinal, and interval. **Nominal data** are data made up of named things (the Latin root of "nominal" is *name*). Another term for nominal data is **categorical data.** This is easy to remember if you think of the data as coming from categories. We will use the more common term, *nominal,* from this point on. As you can see in Table 2–1, nominal data are made up of items that do not have a value attached to them—things that are *not* numbers.

One piece of nominal data cannot be greater or lesser, better or poorer, than any other piece. There is no value attached to a palm tree over an oak. They are simply different. As we discuss below, analyzing nominal data is similar to putting different

Table 2-1 Examples of nominal data

Variable	Data
HIV status	Positive, negative
Tree species	Oak, maple, birch, palm
Sex	Female, male
Nationality	Canadian, American, Mexican, Brazilian
Zoning	Commercial, residential, industrial
Employment status	Employed, unemployed, retired

observations into different boxes and then seeing what patterns emerge. The numbers in the categories may be fewer or greater; you might have more retired neighbors than employed neighbors. But retired is not "better" than employed (at least not in theory). As you will see later, with some types of statistical analysis we may code different categories with a 1 or a 0, but that is only to allow the computer to read our data, not to apply values to them.

The best analyses combine all three types of information: nominal, ordinal, and interval.

The next type of data is ordinal. **Ordinal data** are also made up of names, or categories, but as you can see in Table 2–2, these data can be ranked: that is, we *can* say that one piece is higher or lower, greater or lesser, than another. However, ordinal data do not have specific values, so we cannot measure an exact value between them. For example, I freely admit that my baseball skills are poor, my husband's are fair, and my sons' are excellent. I can put these in order from worse to better, but I cannot really measure the distance between my skill level and that of my husband, or between his skill level and that of my sons!

Table 2-2 Examples of ordinal data

Variable	Data
Condition of the municipal building	Poor, fair, excellent
Level of education completed	Grade school, high school, college, postgraduate
Satisfaction with municipal service	Unsatisfied, neutral, satisfied
Heat in salsa	Mild, medium, hot, red hot fire
Critic's opinion of movies	One star, two stars, three stars

In the last example, you might argue that a movie with two stars is twice as good as a movie with one star, but most movie critics would not be that precise. In fact, that is a good way to describe ordinal data. They give you a sense of the order of items, but they are not precise.

The last type of data, and the type you are probably most familiar with, is interval data, as shown in Table 2–3. **Interval data** are numerical, with equal intervals between values. Interval data are found everywhere in research. In fact, many researchers are uncomfortable working with anything other than interval data. And perhaps, because nominal or ordinal data are often counted and coded into numbers for computers to "read," all data might ultimately be considered interval in natural. However, that is a false conclusion. Interval data alone are precise. The distance between 12 and 13, and 23 and 24, and 12,852 and 12,853 is exactly the same. Also, the interval of 1 can be divided into smaller and smaller equal units.

Table 2-3   Examples of interval data from three cities

Variable	Interval data		
	City 1	City 2	City 3
Department budget subtotals	$82,000	$95,000	$225,000
Vehicles in motor fleet	24	3	45
Parking space size	160 cubic feet	180 cubic feet	175 cubic feet
New employees in FY 2010	16	54	0
Degrees too cold the thermostat is set in the manager's office	2	5	12 (freezing!)

The key characteristic of interval data is precision. And as we learned in the last chapter, the idea of precision is linked to the statistical concept of reliability. But reliable data are not necessarily valid, or what we might think of as accurately capturing a concept. Think about what you see when you step on and off a scale several times. Usually the scale will give you about the same reading, the same number of pounds, each time you step on it. The number of pounds shown each time is interval data. This is a relatively precise measurement. However, does the number of pounds really represent whether someone is fat, skinny, or just right? Obviously not. It is not necessarily, by itself, a valid measure of health or body image. It is only a valid measurement of weight. How we view ourselves is much more complex and cannot be represented by a single number. So while researchers tend to love interval data because they are easy to use with math and computers, in the big picture interval data are limited. Interval data are not any better or worse than nominal or ordinal data; they are just different. Do not mistake the precision of interval data as being a claim to accuracy.

Why do we worry so much about labeling the type of data we are going to use? In the coming chapters you will see that the type of data we have will determine what statistical methods we use. The data are the building blocks of any research. As another reminder of the concepts in the last chapter, good data are those that are both valid and reliable. Nominal and ordinal data can be vague, but they can also better capture a concept. However, because they are not precise, it is much harder to use statistics with them. Interval data are a mathematically inclined scientist's dream, but they can be limited by their precision: they measure a concept in only one defined way. This book talks about statistical methods to use with different kinds of data, but in the big picture, the best analyses combine all three types of information.

Levels of data

When looking at data, you need to know not only what kind they are but also from what level. What does that mean, you ask? If you think about it, the phrase "looking at data" is very appropriate here. In the same way that we might zoom in close with a camera to capture a person's face, or zoom out to capture a whole class, or really zoom out to take a picture of a whole school, we need to understand if our information is from a person, a school, a municipality, a county, a state, or a country. The level of information is called the **unit of analysis.**

When you have gathered information on a number of units (people, schools, departments, cities, etc.), you have what's called a data series (which we'll come back to shortly).

Table 2-4   Examples of data series and units of analysis

Data	Unit of analysis
Salaries of Tom, Dick, and Harry	Individual or person
Weight of Peter, Paul, and Mary	Individual or person
Number of employees for each state	State
Size of municipal parking spaces	Parking space
Average size of municipal parking spaces	Neighborhood, municipality, county, or state

The last two examples in Table 2–4 above are interesting. It is probably obvious that if you have a list of numbers from different parking spaces, the unit of analysis is parking space. However, the next example is not so clear. If you have a list of average parking space sizes, the unit of analysis is the area from which the average parking space size comes. That is, you might have to be specific about whether the average is of all spaces in a neighborhood, a municipality, or a county. The average will have been calculated from individual observations from someone measuring different parking spaces around a town (a fun summer job for an MPA intern, I think), but the average is calculated across the whole town and recorded as the town's average parking space size. There is only one average for all of Council Top, for example. Thus, Council Top, or the municipality, is the unit of analysis.

Variables

When you collect data, you are collecting information on a **variable.** A variable is just a fancy word for a characteristic that varies from observation to observation. For example, height varies across people, and gross national product varies across countries. It may seem obvious, but to do any kind of statistical analysis, you need to have information on variables. This means that the data on a characteristic must vary. But sometimes we forget this simple lesson. If all Girl Scouts are girls, it doesn't make much sense in a study on Girl Scouts to have a variable on sex to determine whether the Girl Scout is a boy or a girl. To take a lesson from my son's homework, you might ask if some kinds of turtles are reptiles and some are not. But all turtles are reptiles! The reptile "status" of turtles doesn't change or vary. In other words, it is not a variable.

It is sometimes easy to fall into the trap of gathering information on a variable that doesn't really vary. In research I was completing on why people visit nonprofit food pantries, I gathered information on whether the individuals had to apply for food stamps. At the first pantry I visited, I duly started to record this information. It was included in the files for the clients. Halfway through the day I realized that every person was recorded as receiving or having applied for food stamps. An inquiry to the pantry director cleared up the situation. This pantry gave assistance *only* if the client was already on or had applied for food stamps, so everyone was! I had wasted time and effort recording information that did not vary. I tried to ease my embarrassment by noting that the client files were also including information that was not necessary, so I was not alone. But then the pantry director told me that the records were also used for federal reporting requirements as part of a grant application, and while it didn't make sense to him, the staff recorded what the government told them to record in order to get the funding. After rethinking my research, I realized that I did not want to capture whether the person had applied for food stamps but whether he or she was actually receiving food stamps. When I revisited the data, there *was* variation, and it became an important factor in the long run.

Variation makes statistics possible. Conducting research with statistics is possible only because you are looking for change—if it happens, where it happens, and why. Another way to think about it is that we are looking for patterns. This is the guiding reason why more pieces of information are generally better than fewer pieces. You can imagine a television screen with few pixels: the picture is not very clear. The more pixels, the sharper the image, the more able you are to tell one object from another. In the same way, the more observations or data points, the clearer we are able to see, say, how training programs influence worker productivity or whether a holiday or a pay increase is the better way to raise employee morale. The more data, the stronger the patterns (if they exist), and the more confident we are in our claims about these patterns.

Variation makes statistics possible. We are looking for patterns.

We should note, however, that at the extreme, an abundance of data can include "white noise." That is, just like a live music recording can include background sounds such as someone in the audience sneezing or the distant roar of a highway, very large data sets, usually containing thousands and thousands of observations, can include some irrelevant information. In those cases, the job of the researchers is to cheer about how much data they have and then take a deep breath before digging in to **clean the data.** Just like a music engineer might clean out the sound of sneezing from the recording, the researcher will clean out problem data points (more on recognizing those later in this chapter) and organize the information so that it can be analyzed. Even after obvious problem data points are cleaned out, there will always be some random variation in the data, and the picture will not be entirely, totally, 20/20 clear. But we try to get as close as possible.

Kinds of data sets

When you have gathered a group or several series of pieces of information, or data, it is called a **data set.** We have talked about understanding what kind of data you want or have. In addition to the type of data (nominal, ordinal, or interval) and the level of data (unit of analysis), you need to understand what kind of data set you have. Data sets are made up of individual **data series**—streams or lists of information, such as the batting record for a baseball player for each of the past 20 years. The individual pieces of information, such as the batting average for that player in 2006, are observations, also called **data points.**

There are three types of data sets. The first type is called **cross-sectional.** Usually, instead of saying that we have a cross-sectional data set, we use shorthand and say that we have cross-sectional data. Cross-sectional data cut across our units of analysis. It is easy to think of this in almost a physical sense. Cross-sectional data cut through, or across, things in a horizontal way; they are collected at one point in time. You might gather data—for example, students' reading scores—across schools, cities, or states. Each observation represents a different place or person, but all observations are gathered simultaneously and compiled into a list of reading scores. Cross-sectional data are the most common type of data used in comparisons. If I were interested in testing my guess (or hypothesis) that rural areas have larger parking spaces than urban areas (adding in population just for fun), I would set up a cross-sectional table like Table 2–5, in which the unit of analysis is the municipality.

Table 2-5   Example of a cross-sectional data set

Municipalities	Size of parking spaces	Rural or urban	Overall population
Municipality 1			
Municipality 2			
Municipality 3			
Municipality 4			
Municipality 5			

The second type of data set is **longitudinal** or **time series.** In the same shorthand we used above, we usually say that we have time-series data, which are the same as time-trend data. Time-series data cut across time. Usually we look at just one or two variables and see how they have changed over time. You might gather data across years, months, weeks, or days to see if you are doing better or worse than at some time in the past. The political question, "Are you better off than four years ago?" is exactly that kind of comparison. The pattern of rising and falling gas prices over the years is another example. If I'm considering moving to Iowa, I might want to know if the economy there (in terms of the gross domestic product, or GDP) is more or less stable over time compared to that of North Carolina and of the country as a whole. My time-series table would look like Table 2–6, in which the unit of analysis is the year.

In this example, I am looking at the same variable (GDP) over time in a couple different locations. This allows me to look at the trends in that variable in different locations

Table 2-6   Example of a time-series data set

Year	Growth in North Carolina GDP	Growth in Iowa GDP	Growth in national GDP
2005			
2006			
2007			
2008			
2009			

so that I can compare the rise and fall of the economy in those locations over the same period. I could also look at the same location but at different variables within it, comparing the rise and fall of different things in the same place over time, as in Table 2–7.

Table 2-7   Another example of a time-series data set

| Year | North Carolina | | |
	Growth in GDP	Growth in population	Growth in sales tax revenues
2005			
2006			
2007			
2008			
2009			

Cross-sectional data are no better or worse than time-series data; they are just different. Whether to gather cross-sectional data or time-series data depends on what question you are asking. The two types of data sets answer different kinds of questions. Cross-sectional data answer the question of how we compare to others. Time-series data answer the question of how we compare to ourselves over time. What if we want to compare ourselves to others over time? A panel data set is the answer. Panel data are cross-sectional data over time. Look first at Table 2–8 and consider: why would it be difficult to do an analysis with this table?

Table 2-8   An example of a troublesome table

Year	Growth in North Carolina GDP	Growth in Iowa population	Growth in national sales tax revenues
2005			
2006			
2007			
2008			
2009			

What gets tricky is when you try to include different years and different variables in the same table. Is Table 2–8 useful? It is set up with the unit of analysis being the year, but the variables are a hodge-podge of things and places.

On the other hand, a panel data set like the one shown in Table 2–9 *can* capture data across both time and location.

Table 2-9   An example of a panel data set

Year/ state	Growth in GDP		Growth in population		Growth in sales tax revenues	
	NC	Iowa	NC	Iowa	NC	Iowa
2005						
2006						
2007						
2008						
2009						

The unit of analysis is year/state so that we have observations on variables for different states in different years. You could also look at state/year if you wanted to, such as in Table 2–10. The computer will read the data in the same way. The computer doesn't care about the labels; it will only look for patterns in the data. The labels are for us so that we can make sure we are gathering the right information to answer the question to solve the problem.

Table 2-10   Another example of a panel data set

State/year	Growth in GDP					Growth in population					Growth in sales tax revenues				
	2005	2006	2007	2008	2009	2005	2006	2007	2008	2009	2005	2006	2007	2008	2009
North Carolina															
Iowa															

Chuck took a quick glance at his reflection in the windows looking over

the parking lot. He wasn't particularly self-conscious, but ever since the meetings were put on public access television, he had at least tried to not embarrass himself. Did his wide tie make him look fat? He tried to refocus. Let's see, he thought, what information about inspections could be surprising?

He turned to Nina. "So what is surprising? That our average number of home inspections is not very high compared to Neola's?" asked Chuck, looking down at the agenda and referring to the bustling town about twenty-three miles south to which Council Top was always being compared. One of the council members wanted to know why dilapidated homes on the northeast side were not being forced to clean up, and the issue was on the agenda. That was the only thing he could think of. The inspection staff always reported that it led the county in average number of inspections, but Chuck didn't ever see the official numbers.

"That the average number of inspections is not the right number to look at," she replied with a smile.

Review questions

1. What is the difference between observations and data?
2. What type of data is ethnicity? What makes it that type of data?
3. What is an example of ordinal data? What makes it ordinal data?
4. Define the term *variable*.
5. Give an example of a variable and the data that would be examined within that variable.
   Example: Sex (variable): female, male (data)
6. What type of variable is each of the following:
   a. Tax I.D. number
   b. Weight
   c. Number of parking spaces
   d. Satisfaction level
   e. Nationality
   f. Employment status
7. Define and give an example of cross-sectional data.
8. What is the difference between unit of analysis and data series? Give examples of each.
9. Give examples of both cross-sectional and longitudinal data sets.
10. Find an example of panel data. How are they organized?

Bring Some Order to This Chaos!

3

[MORE DESCRIPTIVE STATISTICS]

Nina approached the microphone at the front of the room and stood next to Chuck. This was her first time addressing the council, and while outwardly she appeared calm, inside she was nervous. She tried to reassure herself that she was well prepared. She herself had typed every one of these numbers into her spreadsheet, and knew them better than anyone else in the room.

Chuck started. "Item 5 on our agenda is the home inspections data review. Last week, in our open comment time, a citizen raised her concerns about the poor condition of houses in the most southern part of Ginger Street. She suggested that the city was not keeping up with home inspections the way it should, comparing us to Neola, which she felt had a good record of home inspections. Council asked my office to explore the issue. In response, Nina Schorn, our new analyst, has prepared a short briefing on the home inspections data. Nina?" said Chuck.

"Thank you, Mr. Edwards. Let me first tell you a little about how we gather the inspections data, and then I'll review some basic descriptive information. Every week, our inspectors conduct dozens of inspections. The department is experimenting with an electronic system in which inspectors will have laptops with them and will record the inspection information directly into their laptops. The information will be downloaded twice a day into a central department database. This will allow for much easier and quicker recording, tracking, and analysis of the data. Unfortunately, the system has a number of bugs in it, and the only person who knows how to run the preset reports on it is on extended disability leave." The eyes of a couple of council members rolled. The portly woman on the end of the council table stifled a laugh. The chair, Leo Berner, was smiling. Leo always smiled.

Nina took a deep breath and continued. "However, I took the past year's data from the paper records on file and entered them into a spreadsheet. And there are some interesting findings when we compare ourselves to Neola."

"I'm almost afraid to ask," interrupted the portly woman, "but how are we doing on average compared to those rapscallions?"

"Last year," said Nina, "we reported that in a typical week, 24 inspections were done, compared to an average of 43 in Neola, but...."

"Twenty four compared to 43? That's shameful! What's wrong with our inspection program?" the woman demanded, turning to Chuck.

"I'll speak to the department head this week and ask for an explanation," said Chuck, turning to look at the department head, who was shaking his head. "I'll report back to you personally this week–," he hurried to say.

"You don't need to," said Nina loudly. When the room got quiet, she went on. "You don't need to; I can explain it easily. You see, 24 is the wrong number to use here. That's the mode. We need to look at the median." The department head looked very relieved.

"What is the mode? Or the median for that matter? I just want what is typical. How about the average?" said Leo.

"In this case, that would be close," she replied, "but it's still not the best way to think of a typical week for our inspections department." Nina clicked on her PowerPoint and started to explain.

S tatistics are used in two ways: (1) to describe a thing or phenomenon and (2) to infer something about that thing or phenomenon. So it is not a surprise that there are two types of statistics: **descriptive** and **inferential**. This chapter deals with the first part of descriptive statistics.

If something looks odd, it probably is.

Descriptive statistics are the basis, the foundation, for *everything else* in any kind of analysis. If we don't have descriptive statistics, we cannot do any other type of analysis. Yet we often give descriptive statistics short shrift. Averages don't sound exciting unless, perhaps, they are used in baseball; fashion mode is a better conversation starter than numerical mode. Students and well-meaning professionals often run to impress others by whipping up a multivariate regression (something you, too, will be able to do by the time you get to the end of this book). However, rushing into something complicated without understanding the basics is a recipe for disaster.

One time I made brownies at my brother's house. My mom, brother, and I were visiting him for the weekend. Tired from the long drive, we rented a movie and settled in for the evening. I had a strong desire for something sweet. My brother, a law student at the time, had a box mix for brownies. It had been bought recently, but unfortunately, the vegetable oil in the back of the shelf had not. The immediate lesson I learned that night is that brownies made with rancid oil do not taste good. The larger lesson is that if you do not pay attention to all the ingredients of a recipe, the result can stink. Same with statistics. You need to make sure that all the ingredients—or, in this case, the data—are good before combining them. Otherwise, one bad addition can throw off the whole batch. In a kitchen, if you get a whiff of something that smells bad, it probably is bad. In statistics, if something looks odd, it probably is odd. In both cases, you need to examine everything to see what is actually going on.

How many? Counts/frequency distributions

Let's return to Nina's problem. The council had asked her to examine the data on house inspections. Table 3–1 shows the data she obtained by week for one year.

The absolute first step in any kind of data analysis is to look at the information. With interval data, when we just look at all the numbers, it is hard to get a clear

Table 3-1 Housing inspections data for Council Top, 20xx

Week in the year	No. of inspections	Week in the year	No. of inspections	Week in the year	No. of inspections	Week in the year	No. of inspections
1	12	14	23	27	52	40	48
2	21	15	100	28	67	41	37
3	19	16	52	29	89	42	36
4	29	17	41	30	74	43	34
5	29	18	78	31	83	44	32
6	27	19	45	32	99	45	62
7	49	20	28	33	84	46	35
8	66	21	0	34	75	47	13
9	80	22	37	35	74	48	15
10	64	23	75	36	81	49	29
11	66	24	89	37	73	50	12
12	37	25	79	38	91	51	5
13	68	26	80	39	83	52	0

picture of the information as a whole. As the famous phrase says, a picture is worth a thousand words, er..., data points. Our next step may be to literally make a picture: a graph. Figure 3–1 is a simple Excel graph of the number of inspections over the year.

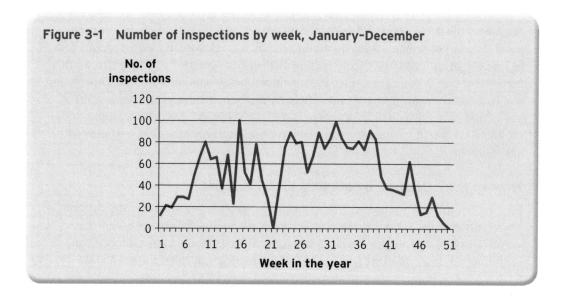

Figure 3-1   Number of inspections by week, January-December

The information is still hard to read. What stands out? At the beginning of the year, inspections start out slowly; they then increase in the middle of the year before dropping off again. If home inspections follow home construction patterns, the dropoff makes sense. When the weather is better in Council Top, more home construction takes place. Yet something is strange: the observations around week 21 take a nosedive. And as we said, if something looks unusual, it probably is. In this case, we would call the observation an **outlier:** that is, it lies outside of the normal pattern of the data.

If I had these data, I would want to know why they took such a steep drop in the 20th and 21st weeks before rebounding up in week 22. I can find this out only by actually going back to the original data and asking questions. First, was there a typo or mistake in the data? Sometimes those types of mistakes are obvious, and you can legitimately correct the data. But if you are not sure it is a mistake, you must assume that the data are correct and that something else is coming into play. Did something unusual happen in those weeks?

Luckily, when Nina looked into the actual data, she found her answer. The department data were correct. There are two inspectors in the department. In weeks 20 and 21, one of the inspectors took his annual vacation. In weeks 21 and 22, the other inspector took her vacation. This left the department effectively half-staffed for the first week, closed for the middle week when both inspectors were on vacation, and half-staffed again for the third week. So during these three weeks, this small department was not operating normally.

What should be done with outliers like these? There are three options. First, if there is an obvious typo or entry mistake, you can correct the item and note the correction. Second, you can keep all observations in the data set, including the outliers, so that they have as much **weight,** or impact, as any other piece of data. This would be the position of data purists, who decline to change any aspect of a data set for fear of introducing bias. The benefit of keeping the outlier in is that no one can accuse you of manipulating the data set. Also, unless you know why there is an outlier (such as the staff not being in the department), you do not have a legitimate basis for throwing it out. If the department were fully staffed and we could not identify anything else going on, we would note that it was an outlier but probably keep it in our analysis. The "cost" of keeping the data point in is that it will alter, or skew, our data analysis because it is so different from all the other data points. (More about skew later.)

Third, you can exclude, or throw out, the outlier, arguing that it is not representative of the true pattern of the data. In this case, the benefit is that the "normal" pattern is clearer. The cost is that we, as analysts, have used our subjective judgment to throw the data point out, and therefore we can be accused of manipulating the results.

As a practitioner, I recommend that you not try to be a data purist. Throw out extreme outliers if, after determining *why* they are outliers, you don't feel that they represent the true nature of what you are examining. What if you are not sure whether throwing out an outlier would be legitimate? Take both approaches! Show your information and analysis both with and without the outliers, and let the audience be the judge. Figure 3–2 shows the same information but without the three outliers identified above.

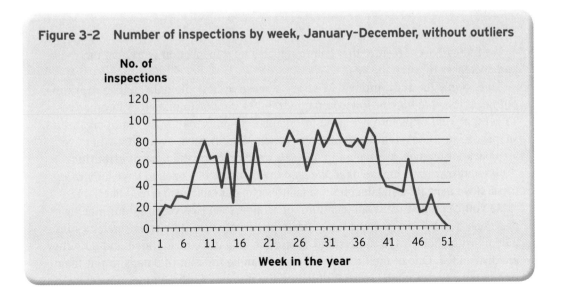

Figure 3-2   Number of inspections by week, January–December, without outliers

You can even take this process one step further by **smoothing the data** so that the graph shows the general patterns without all the individual spikes and valleys. To do this, we simply add a trend line through the data, as shown in Figure 3–3. The trend line is made by creating a new data series of **moving averages**—in this case, where each point is the average of five years' of values: the point in the middle, plus the two years before and the two years after. Luckily, most spreadsheet software packages can add trend lines with a keystroke, and you can customize your trend line to be straight or curved, a moving average of any number of years, or any other type of line. The more years you use to create the moving average, the smoother the data line becomes.

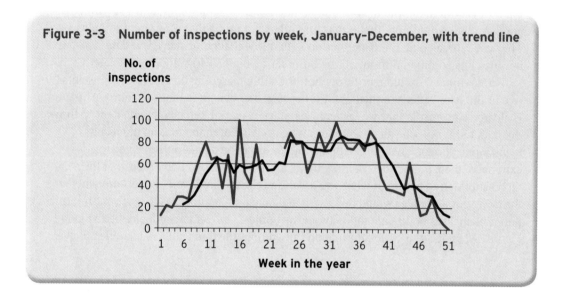

Figure 3-3   Number of inspections by week, January-December, with trend line

We finally have a picture that communicates how inspection workload increases and decreases through the year.

This is only the start, though. We have a sense of how the data change over time, but not if they are high or low compared to other data or to ourselves in other years. To get that kind of picture, we need to organize the information so that it creates a snapshot—just like a television organizes each pixel in such a way that when we step back far enough, we see an image. We need to know the **data distribution.**

We start by organizing the data. We tend to organize from small to large, or vice versa. If we reorganize the data from small to large, our table would read like Table 3–2.

As you can tell, a really long column of numbers isn't very helpful for making decisions, either. This is the value of descriptive statistics. Descriptive statistics provide us with shortcuts to understand where the data are concentrated and how they are distributed. One of the first ways to get a handle on a lot of data is to put them into groups. For example, instead of listing the number 37 three times above, we can

Table 3-2   Home inspections by week

Week in the year	No. of inspections	Week in the year	No. of inspections	Week in the year	No. of inspections	Week in the year	No. of inspections
21	0	5	29	16	52	18	78
52	0	49	29	27	52	25	79
51	5	44	32	45	62	9	80
1	12	43	34	10	64	26	80
50	12	46	35	8	66	36	81
47	13	42	36	11	66	31	83
48	15	12	37	28	67	39	83
3	19	22	37	13	68	33	84
2	21	41	37	37	73	24	89
14	23	17	41	30	74	29	89
6	27	19	45	35	74	38	91
20	28	40	48	23	75	32	99
4	29	7	49	34	75	15	100

shorten the list by inserting all the unique numbers and how often they occur, or their **frequency.** With that, our table might look like Table 3–3.

We have now moved from a graduated list of the number of weekly inspections to a **frequency distribution.** In this case, the frequency distribution is not much of an

Table 3-3   Frequency table of home inspections

No. of inspections	Frequency	No. of inspections	Frequency	No. of inspections	Frequency	No. of inspections	Frequency
0	2	29	3	52	2	79	1
5	1	32	1	62	1	80	2
12	2	34	1	64	1	81	1
13	1	35	1	66	2	83	2
15	1	36	1	67	1	84	1
19	1	37	3	68	1	89	2
21	1	41	1	73	1	91	1
23	1	45	1	74	2	99	1
27	1	48	1	75	2	100	1
28	1	49	1	78	1		

improvement over the really long column; the difference between some of these numbers (say, 89 and 91 inspections) is not that great. We could easily collapse the data into groups—for example, boxes representing "tens"— to produce Table 3–4.

You'll see that in addition to the frequency distribution, I included a **percentage distribution.** For each group of tens, we calculated the number of weeks out of the total that fell into that group. For example, there were

Table 3-4   Frequency distribution table

No. of inspections	Frequency distribution (no. of weeks)	Percentage distribution (% of total weeks)
0–10	3	5.7
11–20	5	9.6
21–30	7	13.5
31–40	7	13.5
41–50	4	7.7
51–60	2	3.9
61–70	6	11.5
71–80	7	13.5
81–90	8	15.4
91–100	3	5.7

three weeks in which the number of inspections was between 0 and 10. These three, divided by the total number of weeks (52), equals 5.7%. In this way, we were able to determine where the bulk of our observations fall. From Table 3–4 it can be seen that Council Top's inspection department did between 51 and 60 inspections a week in two separate weeks, or nearly 4% of the year; however, it did between 31 and 40 inspections a week in seven separate weeks, or 13.5% of the year.

A percentage distribution table allows us to be even more specific: we can determine where the bottom 25% and top 25% of observations fall. We can tell what point is in the exact middle: the point at which 50% of the weeks (26) had a lower number of inspections and at which 50% of the weeks had a higher number of inspections. In this case, it is 41–50. One half of the weeks had 40 or fewer inspections, and one half had 41 or more. The major break points, which are at 25%, 50%, and 75%, are called **quartiles,** meaning that each represents a quarter of all the data points. From the top of the lower quartile to the bottom of the upper quartile (from 25% of observations to 75% of observations) is called the **interquartile range** since it represents the inner portion, or middle section of observations.

Frequency distributions are great tools to use because you can also take any particular value and find out what percentage of observations lies above that number and what percentage lies below it. Table 3–5, for example, is the same table as above, but now it includes a cumulative frequency distribution and cumulative percentage distribution.

In Figure 3–3 we saw our data visually with a trend-line chart. We can also see data visually with a **histogram,** as shown in Figure 3–4. If Nina presented this chart to the council, she would be able to communicate a lot of information in a single figure. A simple look suggests that the data are in two main groups, a higher group and

Table 3-5   Frequency, cumulative frequency, percentage, and cumulative percentage distributions

No. of inspections	Frequency distribution (no. of weeks)	Cumulative frequency distribution	Percentage distribution (% of total weeks)	Cumulative percentage distribution
0–10	3	3	5.7	5.7
11–20	5	8	9.6	15.3
21–30	7	15	13.5	28.8
31–40	7	22	13.5	42.3
41–50	4	26	7.7	50.0
51–60	2	28	3.9	53.9
61–70	6	34	11.5	65.4
71–80	7	41	13.5	78.9
81–90	8	49	15.4	94.3
91–100	3	52	5.7	100.0

a lower group, but that a typical value might be in the middle. But what do we mean by a "typical" value? That question takes us to the next section: measures of central tendency. But first, a lesson in having too much information. To the histogram below, you can add the cumulative percentages as shown in Figure 3–5.

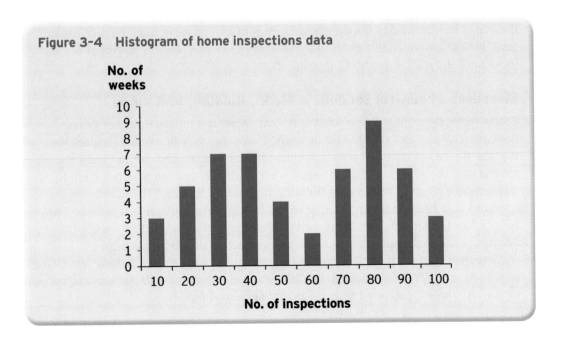

Figure 3-4   Histogram of home inspections data

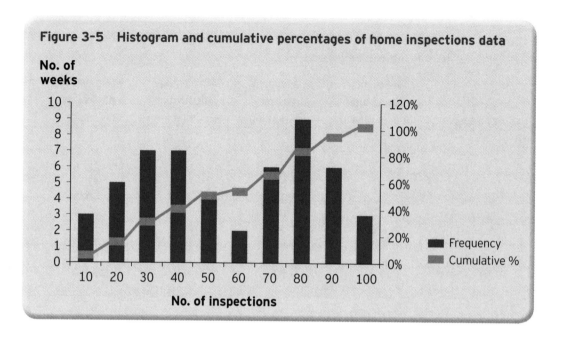

Figure 3-5   Histogram and cumulative percentages of home inspections data

I do not recommend using this kind of graph with too many audiences: it can get confusing quickly. The bars represent the number of weeks when there were up to 10, 11–20, 21–30, etc., home inspections. The line represents how each group adds to the total percentage. A place where the line is steep represents that the number of weeks in that range is a lot relative to the total number of weeks. A place where the line is flat means that the number of weeks in that range is small relative to the total. If Nina presented this chart to the council, she would likely get a lot of blank looks until she walked members through it.

Measures of central tendency: Mean, median, and mode

People generally want to know what is typical. What is a typical day like? What does a typical citizen look like? What would I expect to find in a typical house? We capture the idea of "typical" with a couple different values. First, we put bookends around our data—or, in statistical terms, we first identify the **range** of our data. In this case, the range of values goes from a couple weeks in which the number of inspections was 10 or under to a couple weeks in which the number was close to 100. Specifically, the range is the difference between the lowest and highest values (here, between a low of 0 inspections in one week and a high of 100 in another).

That gives us the top and bottom, but we are still looking for the typical value. Of course, in statistics, things have to be difficult. There are three different ways to be typical. All three are referred to as **measures of central tendency.**

First, we look for the **average**—or, in statistical terms, the **mean.** The terms *mean* and *average* are the same thing. To calculate the mean, one adds up all the values in a data series and divides by the number of values. In our running example, you add up all the number of inspections from all the weeks, and then divide by the number of weeks, or 52. If you want to impress your friends at lunch, you could casually draw the formula for the mean on a napkin:

$$\mu = (\Sigma X)/N,$$

where μ is the Greek letter mu, the notation for "mean"

Σ is the notation for "sum of"

X is the notation for a variable—usually, a series of numbers

N is the number of numbers.

The average is probably the most widely used descriptive statistic. However, it is probably also the most misused. Averages work really well when data are normally distributed. We'll discuss normal distribution much more in the coming chapters, but for right now, you can imagine a normal curve as a bell-like curve such as the one in Figure 3–6, where most values are in the middle, some are at the high end, and some at the low end.

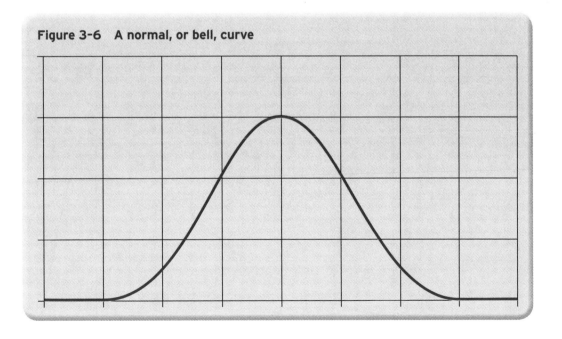

Figure 3-6   A normal, or bell, curve

However, averages can change dramatically with a single or a few numbers in the series that are very high or very low relative to the rest of the numbers. Average income in the state of Washington, for example, may not be a good measure of the income of a typical person in a random Washington town. Why? Well, Bill Gates, the multibillionaire of Microsoft computer fame, lives there. His income would shift the average from what is considered typical to a higher number. The same would be said of Warren Buffett, Bill's billionaire friend in Omaha, Nebraska. Average income in the city would be much higher if Buffett's income were included in the calculation. In our running example of home inspections, the weeks when the inspectors were on vacation and the number of inspections was zero are clearly not typical inspection weeks. Those values of zero pull the average down lower than a typical week would represent. When you have these types of extreme values, we say the data are **skewed.**

Bill Gates's income can really "skew" things up.

Like everyone else, statisticians like to have a sense of the data in a picture, so when they hear that data are skewed, they know it really means "screwed up by outliers." More importantly, they want to know *how* the data are skewed: is the outlier on the high end or on the low end? If it is on the high end, the curve is stretched out to the right, in a positive direction, to include the outlier. In this case, as shown in Figure 3–7, the data distribution has a **positive skew.** If the outliers are on the low

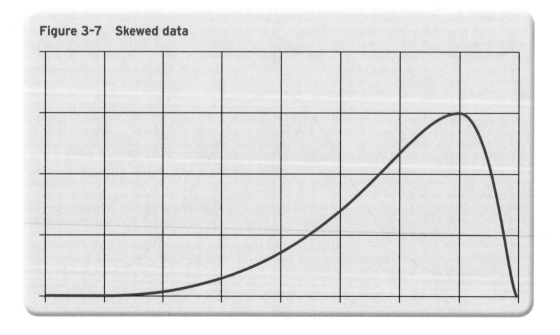

Figure 3-7   Skewed data

end, the curve is stretched out to the left, or in a negative direction, in which case the data distribution has a **negative skew.**

If we cannot use the average, then, how else can we measure what would be the typical value of a data series? An alternative would be the **median**—literally, the middle value. The median is the value above which and below which 50% of the data series falls. If your data series were 1, 2, 3, 4, and 5, the median would be the number 3 because half of the other numbers (numbers 1 and 2) fall below it and the other half (numbers 4 and 5) fall above it. The median is easy to identify in a data set that comprises an odd number of observations, or data points, because there is a middle number. If there is an even number of data points, however, there is not a value that falls in the exact middle. In that case, the median is halfway between the middle two values. Thus, if our data series were 1, 2, 3, 4, 5, and 6, the median would be 3.5.

Whenever there are outliers in data, researchers tend to use the median as a typical value rather than the average. This is why median income is often used instead of average income in analyses. The same logic applies to median house value or property tax bill or utility bill: in all cases, the average could easily be skewed by extremely low or high values.

> If there are extreme values in your data set, use the median instead of the mean.

So is the median the best measure of a typical value; that is, does it best show where the central bulk of the data lie? Not always. Medians can also fool us, although it is less likely. If you look back at our distribution of inspection data in Figure 3–4, you'll see that there are really two different clusters of data, not one. In this case, the median would not be a good example of a typical value. Our data represent a bi-model distribution—more like two normal curves next to each other. So, like the average, there are times when the median is not the best to use.

What is left? The **mode.** The mode represents the most common single value—in other words, the value that occurs most frequently. In our data, the mode is in the 80s; that is, we had more weeks when the number of housing inspections was in the 80s than weeks in any other category. But just like the median, the mode focuses on one value, and that value might not really represent what is going on with the data. In Figure 3–7, the mode would ignore the fact that there is a large cluster of weeks in which the number of inspections was more in the range of 30 or 40.

The average, median, and mode all have strengths and weaknesses when used as the sole piece of information on central tendency or to show what a typical value is. If the mean is higher than the median, you know that there is an outlier with a high value skewing the curve in a positive direction. If the mean is lower than the median, you know that there is an outlier with a low value skewing the curve in a negative direction. If the mode is different from the mean and median, again, there is some skew to the data. But put the mean, the median, and the mode together, and they can be very powerful. Together, they can tell you a lot about the distribution of your data. For example, there is only one case in which the mean = the median = the mode, and it occurs in a normal curve!

The power of simply taking the raw data and organizing it is clear. We can easily get a visual of how the data are distributed simply by knowing the characteristics of the data distribution or basic histogram. More importantly, we can show this information through a whole series of different graphs. In addition to the graphs shown above, another helpful descriptive statistical graph is the **box and whiskers plot.** In this depiction, a box is around the middle two quartiles of data, from 25% to 75%, and the two whiskers are the end points of the data that stretch out from the ends of the box. They represent the bottom and top quartiles. If the whisker on one side is stretched out longer than that on the other, it means that the data are stretched out in that direction. The average is the white line in the middle of the box. With our data on home inspections, excluding the weeks when both inspectors were on vacation, the box and whiskers plot looks like Figure 3–8.

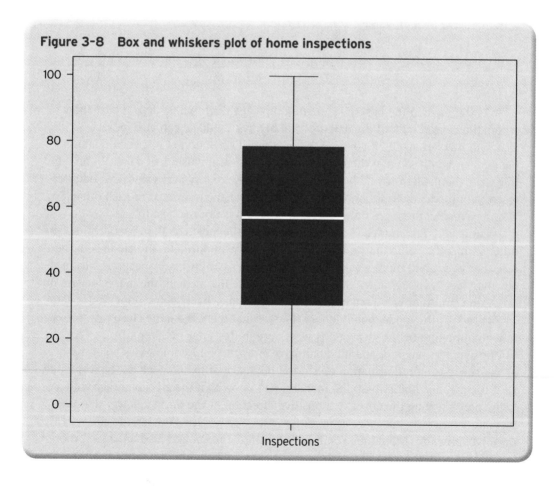

Figure 3-8   Box and whiskers plot of home inspections

So far, from the first graph showing the trend over the year to the box and whiskers plot showing the distribution of the data, we can provide our elected officials with the following information for home inspections in Council Top:

- The number of inspections varied a great deal, between 5 and 100 inspections per week. Generally, the department was able to conduct from about 30 to 80 inspections per week. The median number of inspections was around 50.

- There were two weeks when no inspections were done, but this was Christmas week and a week in the spring when both inspectors were on vacation. Two other weeks, only one inspector was on duty.

- The number of inspections was lower in the winter, but it went up dramatically in the spring and peaked in the middle to late summer/early fall.

You will notice that I used the terms *about* and *around*. That is not because I don't know the exact numbers; in fact it is easy, with a touch of a button in spreadsheet software programs, to find out the basic descriptive statistics down to multiple decimal points. But don't be dazzled by data. Precision to the *n*th degree is generally not the hallmark of good statistical communicators. Nobel Prize–winning economists are often those who can put complex behavior into simple, easily understood terms. For the individual data (again, including only the weeks when both inspectors were on duty), the descriptive data are shown in Table 3–6.

Table 3-6   Home inspections, by week, FY 20xx, using individual data

Statistic	Value
Number of weeks included in analysis	48
Minimum	5
Maximum	100
Range	95 (5 to 100)
Mean	54
Median	57
Mode	29, 37

One difference you might note in the data in Table 3–6 compared with some of the data reported above is that here, the mode of the individual data points is 29 or 37: that is, the values of 29 and 37 each appear three times in our original data set. But that is misleading: when the data points are grouped into tens, the mode is different. There were eight weeks when the number of home inspections was between 81 and 90. There were also seven weeks when the number of home inspections was between 21 and 30, seven when the number was between 31 and 40, and seven more when the number was between 71 and 80. When in doubt, show the picture. Then you don't need to say much else.

Nina finished up, having been concise, concrete, and free of ambiguity, just as she had been taught in her public administration program.

"So we used the wrong number last year?" Councilperson Bendlin didn't sound too surprised.

"I never did understand where that number came from. It seemed far too low to us," the department manager said.

"Well, for some reason, I feel we won't have the same problem this year," Chuck said, looking at Nina with a slight smile.

Review questions

1. Why are the statistics in this chapter called descriptive?

2. What would be a reason to use descriptive statistics? Give examples of possible uses.

3. What is an outlier, and how can it affect data?

4. Give the three ways to deal with an outlier in a data set. What would be the effect of each?

5. What would a data purist do with an outlier and why?

6. When would it be appropriate to use a moving average?

7. From what you've seen in the various tables and charts in this chapter, if you were to hire a part-time temporary employee to help with home inspections, during what time of year would you hire someone? For how many months? Justify your answer.

8. Why is Figure 3-8 called a box and whiskers plot?

9. Describe each of the measures of central tendency and how it is calculated:

    a. Mean

    b. Median

    c. Mode

10. In a data set, if the mean is lower than the median, what can we say about the data?

The Picture Is Becoming Clearer

4

[YET *MORE* DESCRIPTIVE STATISTICS]

Chuck saw the light on in Nina's office when he was walking out Thursday night. "How come you're staying late?"

"Remember the presentation of the inspections data last month?"

"Yeah, you were the talk of the council! At least until Wednesday, when the sewer backed up in the city jail."

"Well, after that, the budget director asked me to do some research on debt at both the state and local levels. At first I didn't think it would be a big deal, but it's more complicated than you think." Nina sounded tired, but you couldn't mistake the underlying interest in her voice. "I just have the state data right now. You see, first I had to find out where to get the data—the budget director wants information on general obligation debt—and then I had to understand whether general obligation debt was defined the same way in each state. You can't mix apples and oranges, you know, or it screws up the entire analysis." Nina wasn't looking at Chuck anymore; she was flipping through her spreadsheets. Her words picked up speed, and Chuck knew she was "in the zone"— what he called it when she was focused and excited about her information.

"I started to come up with a lot of states that didn't have any GO debt at all. Zero. Like Arizona. I thought it was just being very fiscally responsible at first, but actually, Arizona prohibits the use of general obligation debt. So I realized I first had to find out what states are statutorily allowed to carry GO debt, and then look at their debt levels."

"That's good, Nina," said Chuck, as he edged toward the door. Nina didn't seem to notice. She went on, "But once you get the right data and the right states and the right organization, you see some great stuff."

"Great. Well, I have to go home to catch the news—"

"But of course, if you just look at total debt levels by state, you realize that some big states have a lot of debt, and some smaller states have a small amount of debt, and it is more than likely just a function of the state size. So I have to control for that by putting the data into per capita terms."

Chuck couldn't help himself. "What does 'per capita terms' mean?"

"Per person. And when you do that, you see how spread out the data are. You get this." Nina swiveled the computer screen so Chuck could see it in the doorway.

"Wow—and where are we?" Chuck stepped back into the room.

In the last chapter we talked about measures of central tendency—primarily the mean, median, and mode. But knowing the center point of your data is like only seeing someone's bellybutton. You have no idea what the entire person really looks like. We need to see the whole form.

We got the outline of that form through other measures discussed in the last chapter: the range, which tells us the lowest and highest numbers, and the quartiles—the numbers that sit at the 25th, 50th, and 75th percentile points of the data. We even saw how a box and whiskers plot can illustrate the form of the data along one direction. The "picture" of the data is getting better all the time!

However, our form is missing something important: how spread out are the data, relative to the scale we are using?

Standard deviation/measures of dispersion

In statistical terms, measures of spread in the data are called **measures of dispersion.** The most important of these is the **standard deviation.** The standard deviation is so important that instead of just telling you how to interpret it, we are going to actually walk you through how it is calculated so that you have a true sense of what it represents.

> How spread out are your data? The spread serves as the foundation of statistics from this point on.

Standard deviation is vital to understanding all statistics from this point forward. It is the foundation of how we understand whether our data are unusual. Think about it. If our data are all tightly clustered around a central data point and the next data point is far away from that cluster, as shown in Figure 4–1, our impulse is to say that the new data point is unusual.

However, if our data are spread out widely around a central point, a new data point that is far from the central point, as shown in Figure 4–2, does not seem so unusual. The rest of statistics is based on this idea: is a single observation or group of observations different from the rest or from a comparison group? For example, if

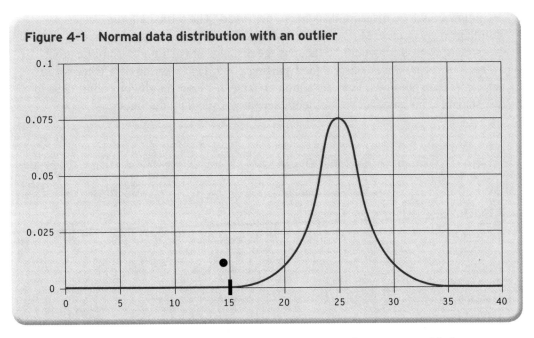

Figure 4-1   Normal data distribution with an outlier

you study really hard for an exam and you score 85 out of 100, you could cheer or cry; it all depends on how everyone else did and where you are relative to the rest. That, in turn, depends on whether the scores are all over the place or tightly clustered around a central place.

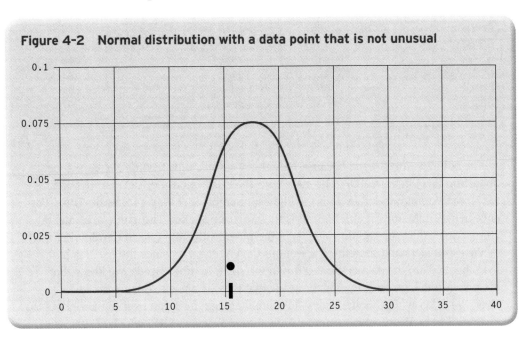

Figure 4-2   Normal distribution with a data point that is not unusual

So how could we measure dispersion, or spread? The term *standard deviation* should give you a clue. Most students, when asked this question, suggest that a good measure of dispersion would be the average distance of each point from the group average, or mean. Sounds like a good starting point. Let's use the data Nina has on per capita debt amounts. First, let's look at Table 4–1 and identify our other descriptive statistics: measures of central tendency, mean, median, and mode.

Table 4–1   General obligation (GO) debt per capita, thirty-seven states, 2007

State	GO debt per capita ($)	State	GO debt per capita ($)
Virginia	117	Pennsylvania	663
Missouri	117	Wisconsin	704
Michigan	148	Minnesota	729
Alabama	167	Vermont	736
New York	173	Nevada	766
Tennessee	181	Georgia	806
Montana	217	Louisiana	896
New Mexico	227	Mississippi	1,074
Texas	283	Maryland	1,113
New Jersey	330	California	1,375
Maine	341	Delaware	1,512
Arkansas	343	Illinois	1,623
West Virginia	411	Washington	1,789
Utah	468	Massachusetts	2,711
South Carolina	502	Connecticut	3,026
New Hampshire	540	Hawaii	3,179
Alaska	592		
Oregon	623	Range	3,062
North Carolina	651	Mean	823
Florida	658	Median	651
Ohio	661	Mode	117

The count is thirty-seven because only thirty-seven states recorded having general obligation (GO) debt in 2007. The state with the least amount of GO debt per capita, $117, was Virginia; the state with the highest amount, $3,179, was Hawaii. The difference between the lowest and highest is the range, or $3,062. The average, or mean, is $823. The median, or middle value, is at the nineteenth state (North Carolina) at $651.

We can understand something about our data right away: since the mean is higher than the median, the data is skewed out to the right. In other words, we know that there are some high outliers, which means that there is a positive skew to the data. How do we know that? Some high values are dragging the mean over to the right of the median. The mode, the most commonly occurring value, is $117, which occurs twice.

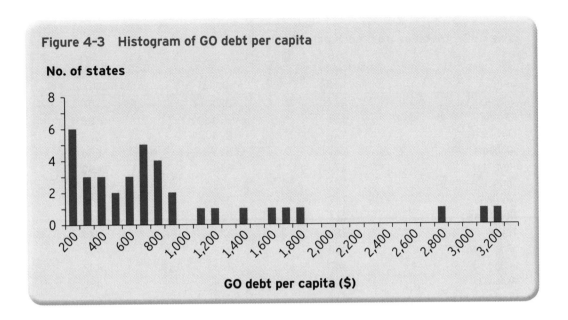

Figure 4-3   Histogram of GO debt per capita

What does the histogram of this data look like? A few clicks in a statistics program will show you. As you can see in Figure 4–3, most states are on the left, with GO debt per capita below $1,000. But some states have very high GO debt per capita—over $2,700! Hawaii has the most at $3,179, but Connecticut and Massachusetts are close behind at $3,026 and $2,711, respectively. With these data, we would want to use the median as a measure of central tendency, not the mean.

Are the data spread out or clustered around the median? Spread out. But how spread out, really? We need the standard deviation now. Remember how we said above that most students, when asked how one might measure spread, start with the average distance from each point to the mean. Okay, how do we get this? We have to calculate how far each point is from the mean (see Table 4–2), total the differences, and take the average.

But when we try to take the average of the distances, what happens? The distances total to zero! It is not surprising, actually. Since the mean is the average, it is, on average, equidistant from all the points! So our gut reaction to take the average distance from the mean is not right. At least, the calculation doesn't work. But perhaps the idea is correct....

Mathematicians are stubborn. If the idea is right but the calculation doesn't work, mathematicians fall back on a whole series of tricks. There are two ways to make this calculation work. One is to take the absolute value of each number in the third column of Table 4–2. This means taking the positive and negatives away from each. If we made each value an absolute number, added them up, and divided by the number of values, we would have the average absolute distance from the mean.

Table 4-2   Distance from each point to the mean

State	GO debt per capita ($)	Mean ($)	Distance from point to mean ($)
Virginia	117	823	706
Missouri	117	823	706
Michigan	148	823	675
Alabama	167	823	656
New York	173	823	650
Tennessee	181	823	642
Montana	217	823	606
New Mexico	227	823	596
Texas	283	823	540
New Jersey	330	823	493
Maine	341	823	482
Arkansas	343	823	480
West Virginia	411	823	412
Utah	468	823	355
South Carolina	502	823	321
New Hampshire	540	823	283
Alaska	592	823	231
Oregon	623	823	200
North Carolina	651	823	172
Florida	658	823	165
Ohio	661	823	162
Pennsylvania	663	823	160
Wisconsin	704	823	119
Minnesota	729	823	94
Vermont	736	823	87
Nevada	766	823	57
Georgia	806	823	17
Louisiana	896	823	-73
Mississippi	1,074	823	-251
Maryland	1,113	823	-290
California	1,375	823	-552
Delaware	1,512	823	-689
Illinois	1,623	823	-800
Washington	1,789	823	-966
Massachusetts	2,711	823	-1,888
Connecticut	3,026	823	-2,203
Hawaii	3,179	823	-2,356

Even more helpful would be squaring each number so that the negatives go away. (Remember that a negative multiplied by a negative is a positive: the negatives cancel each other out.) In addition, the really high values, either positive or negative, get *huge*. Why is this helpful? Because it gives added weight to those values that are really outliers. This means that if a lot of data points are spread out far from the mean, each of those values has a large impact on our eventual standard deviation. The curves shown in Figures 4–4 and 4–5 have the same absolute distance from the mean, but one curve is obviously more spread out, overall, than the other. This would be reflected in the standard deviation for each curve.

Figure 4-4   Normal curve with wide spread

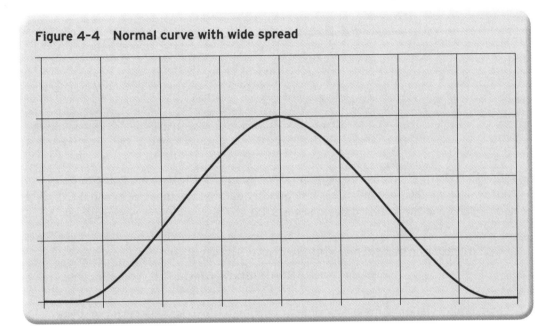

But we still need to get to the standard deviation. We are not there yet. If we square each value, *then* add them up and take the average, we have the average squared deviation from the mean. Now our squaring comes back to haunt us. Since we squared the numbers to make the calculation work in the first place, we need to *unsquare* what we have. In other words, we need to take the square root of the average squared deviation from the mean. And the result is, finally, the standard deviation!

When we put measures of central tendency and measures of dispersion together, we have a great idea of what our data look like. In fact, used together, we can tell whether our data are tightly clustered. If the standard deviation is large relative to the mean, the data are spread out. If the standard deviation is small relative to the mean, the data are tightly clustered. For example, if in one data set the mean per

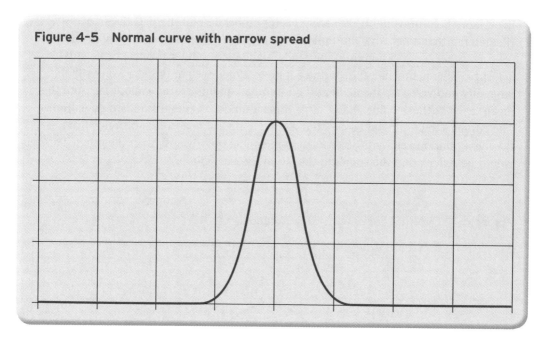

Figure 4-5   **Normal curve with narrow spread**

capita GO debt is $823 and the standard deviation is $8, the data are going to be clustered very tightly around $823. If in another data set the mean per capital GO debt is $823 and the standard deviation is $300, the data will be very spread out.

Standard deviation means nothing just by itself. You have to look at it *with* the mean or median.

Standard deviation is important only in relation to the overall data. If I told you that in a data set hidden behind my back the standard deviation was 7.5, would that mean anything? No. It would only be meaningful if you knew that the mean was 750 or 75. In the first case, the standard deviation would be small compared to the mean, indicating that the data are narrowly clustered. In the second case, the standard deviation would be large compared to the mean, indicating that the data are more spread out. Let's go back to our GO debt per capita table (now Table 4–3).

The standard deviation is the square root of the average of the squared distances from the mean—in this case, $765. To illustrate how the outliers affect the standard deviation, if we take out the three high states (Massachusetts, Connecticut, and Hawaii), our standard deviation drops to $475! This means that these three states are outliers; that is, they are different from the general pattern of the rest of the states. Their extremely high values make the overall distribution much wider—or, in other words, make the standard deviation much larger. In practical use, Nina may

Table 4-3 Distance from each point to the mean, squared, totaled, averaged, and square-rooted (whew!)

State	GO debt per capita ($)	Mean ($)	Distance from point to mean ($)	Distance from point to mean, squared ($)
Virginia	117	823	706	498,436
Missouri	117	823	706	498,436
Michigan	148	823	675	455,625
Alabama	167	823	656	430,336
New York	173	823	650	422,500
Tennessee	181	823	642	412,164
Montana	217	823	606	367,236
New Mexico	227	823	596	355,216
Texas	283	823	540	291,600
New Jersey	330	823	493	243,049
Maine	341	823	482	232,324
Arkansas	343	823	480	230,400
West Virginia	411	823	412	169,744
Utah	468	823	355	126,025
South Carolina	502	823	321	103,041
New Hampshire	540	823	283	80,089
Alaska	592	823	231	53,361
Oregon	623	823	200	40,000
North Carolina	651	823	172	29,584
Florida	658	823	165	27,225
Ohio	661	823	162	26,244
Pennsylvania	663	823	160	25,600
Wisconsin	704	823	119	14,161
Minnesota	729	823	94	8,836
Vermont	736	823	87	7,569
Nevada	766	823	57	3,249
Georgia	806	823	17	289
Louisiana	896	823	-73	5,329
Mississippi	1,074	823	-251	63,001
Maryland	1,113	823	-290	84,100
California	1,375	823	-552	304,704
Delaware	1,512	823	-689	474,721
Illinois	1,623	823	-800	640,000
Washington	1,789	823	-966	933,156
Massachusetts	2,711	823	-1,888	3,564,544
Connecticut	3,026	823	-2,203	4,853,209
Hawaii	3,179	823	-2,356	5,550,736
Total				21,625,839
Average squared deviation				584,482
Square root of average squared deviation of the mean				765

want to exclude these three states from her analysis because their unusual values may be masking the pattern that describes the overall data set much better.

Standard deviation is a very powerful tool. If you have a data set, no matter how large, you calculate out the mean and standard deviation, as well as many, many other more complicated statistics, with a few simple keystrokes in any spreadsheet program. The spreadsheet programs have preprogrammed formulas for any statistic you need, so you can find exactly where any data point is relative to all the other points! Well, I realize this fact may not thrill you, but it is very, very useful in understanding data and doing research. In fact, almost all efforts made to prove something—that a particular medicine works, that military strategy protects a population, or that someone committed a crime—rely on means and standard deviations and the topic of our next section, normal curves.

Whoa! We have talked about means and standard deviations, and a little about normal curves (remember Figure 3–6 on page 37?), but not about how they all work together. Enter the beauty of the *z*-scores and the central limit theorem.

Normal curves

All statisticians will tell you that a normal curve is beautiful. It is shapely, even, and smooth, and looks like a bell. It is symmetrical. It is beautiful because, as shown in Figure 4–6, a couple of mathematical facts exist for *all normal curves:*

- Sixty-eight percent of all data points fall within one standard deviation of the mean.
- Ninety-five percent of all data points fall within two standard deviations of the mean.
- Ninety-nine percent of all data points fall within three standard deviations of the mean.

What does this mean? If you have a complete data set, you have 100% of the data points. If you put a normal curve over this data set, as we did earlier in the book, it will cover 100% of the data points. You can take any point inside that normal curve, and there will be some portion (percentage) above and some portion (percentage) below. The beauty of the standard deviation is that it serves as *a standard measuring stick for us to use with any and every data set*. If you know the mean and standard deviation of a data set, you can find where any value is, from the lowest point to the upper point, on the normal curve. You can do this by measuring, *in standard deviations,* how far that data point is from the mean. Let me illustrate. If we have a normal curve, with a mean of 20 and a standard deviation of 5, I know the following mathematical facts (just using the same facts listed above, with 20 inserted for the mean and 5 inserted for the standard deviation):

- Sixty-eight percent of all data points fall within one standard deviation (5) of the mean (20).

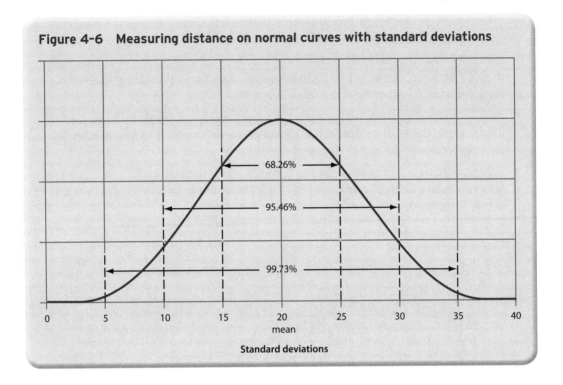

Figure 4-6   Measuring distance on normal curves with standard deviations

- Ninety-five percent of all data points fall within two standard deviations (2 times 5, or 10) of the mean (20).
- Ninety-nine percent of all data points fall within three standard deviations (3 times 5, or 15) of the mean (20).

I can fill in the numbers like this:

- Sixty-eight percent of all data points fall within the value of 20 plus or minus 5.
- Ninety-five percent of all data points fall within the value of 20 plus or minus 10.
- Ninety-nine percent of all data points fall within the value of 20 plus or minus 15.

Then I can fill in the numbers even more completely like this:

- Sixty-eight percent of all data points fall between the values of 15 and 25.
- Ninety-five percent of all data points fall between the values of 10 and 30.
- Ninety-nine percent of all data points fall between 5 and 35.

Because the percentages under any curve have to add up to 100, I also know that if one portion of the curve falls between two numbers in the center, the rest of the curve has to be below or above those numbers. And since the normal curve is symmetrical, whatever is left has to be split between the low end and the high end. With our example, as seen in Figure 4–7, this means:

- If 68% of all data points fall between the values of 15 and 25, then the rest, 32%, are split between values below 15 or above 25. So 16% of the values in the data set are below 15 and 16% of them are above 25.

- If 95% of all data points fall between the values of 10 and 30, then the rest, or 5%, are split between values below 10 and above 30. So 2.5% of the values in the data set are below 10 and 2.5% are above 30.

- If 99% of all data points fall between 5 and 35, then the rest, or only 1%, are split between values below 5 and above 35. So 0.5% of the values in the data set are below 5 and 0.5% are above 35.

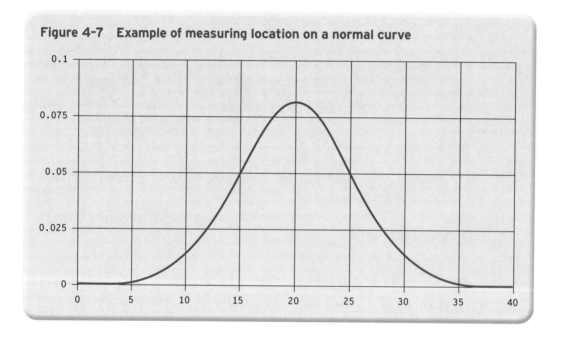

Figure 4-7   Example of measuring location on a normal curve

These facts are the same whether you have a hundred data points in your data set or a million. Right away, if you give me any number, I can tell you about where it falls in my example data set. What about the data point 42? I know 42 is really high, relative to the rest of the data. In fact, I know it is somewhere between the 99th and 100th percentile. What about 8? It is somewhere in the bottom 25th percentile. Try 12. I know right away that it is on the low end of the data set, somewhere between the 95th and 68th percentile point.

The *z*-score

We illustrated how using standard deviations and a normal curve worked with some examples. We can know where every point is by using our measuring stick of standard deviations. Statisticians call this the **z-score.** The *z*-score is the number of standard deviations a particular point is away from the mean in a data set. If I know the mean and the standard deviation, I can calculate a *z*-score for any number in any normally distributed data set. I use the following formula:

$$z = \frac{(\text{data point} - \text{mean})}{\text{standard deviation}}$$

Again, the *z*-score is just a fancy way to measure the distance between the data point and the mean using our measuring stick of standard deviations. What is really cool is that this tool lets us work backward: by knowing the *z*-score, just like in our example above, I know right away about where the data point is relative to the rest of the data set. With a *z*-score that is plus or minus 2 or higher, I know that my data point is somewhere in the upper or lower tail of the data set: if the *z*-score is minus 2 or lower, my data point is in the bottom 2.5% of the curve and almost all the other data points are above it. If the *z*-score is 2 or greater, my data point is in the top 2.5% of the curve and almost all the data points are below it.

Let's illustrate how *z*-scores work with a couple of examples:

Example #1: We could consider how a local government such as Council Top compares to others in the state in terms of police response time. The tricky part of this example is that we would want the response time to be low, meaning that police are arriving quickly. Let's say the average response time across the state is 7.0 minutes. The wonderful spreadsheet program Nina is using calculates the standard deviation of the data set for her, and it is 1.5 minutes. What if Council Top's response time is only 4.0 minutes? Apply these numbers to the formula for scores above. The difference between our data point and the average is 3 minutes. We divide this by the standard deviation, or 1.5 minutes. Council Top's data point has a *z*-score of minus 2; in other words, it is two standard deviations below the average. This tells us that our community is doing well compared to others in the state.

Example #2: To see how our community is doing in terms of education, we can look at a data set of standardized test scores in the state, county, or even grade level. For instance, if we look at elementary schools across the state and our community has a *z*-score of 1, it means that our school's scores are one standard deviation above the mean. This tells us that our community is doing well but has room to improve. To really be at the top of the state in terms of scores, we would want to be two standard deviations above the mean. This would put us in the top 2.5% in the state.

There are two important points to remember about using z-scores. First, when applying the formula above, you need to use the mean and standard deviation either (1) for a **population,** if you have observations for a full population, or for every individual unit, such as all fifty states, or all people in the municipality, or all students in a school; or (2) for a **sample,** such as a subset of states, or a sample of people in the municipality, or a sample of students in each grade. I point this out because the calculation for standard deviation is slightly different for a sample than it is for a population. (The difference between population and sample is discussed further Chapter 6.)

I assume that you will not be calculating a standard deviation by hand but using a spreadsheet. Make sure that you use the appropriate formula.

> ## The calculation for standard deviation is slightly different for a sample than it is for a population.

Second, we need to assume that the curve is normal—in other words, that the data are normally distributed in the form of a bell-shaped curve. All the z-scores and accompanying percentages under the curve, such as 95% of the observations falling within two standard deviations of the mean, are based on a bell-shaped curve. If we do not have a bell-shaped curve distribution, we can't use z-scores.

Well, you might think, "Okay, if this is true, this is *really* helpful. Not. How often do normal curves just appear in data in real life?" Luckily, more often than you think. For example, imagine the heights of all the people in your town. Some are tall. A few are very tall. Some are short. A few are very short. But most fall in between. With thousands of observations, the distribution of heights across an entire city usually falls into a normal curve. This same phenomenon appears with many other characteristics in nature.

More importantly, we can still use z-scores with almost any set of sample data, even if the population distribution is skewed. How? Through the beauty of the central limit theorem.

The central limit theorem

> *The distribution of an average tends to be normal, even when the distribution from which the average is computed is not.*

Huh?

We often encounter skewed distributions in statistics. Earlier in this book, I used the example of how Michael Jordon's income skewed the average income of geography majors from the University of North Carolina at Chapel Hill. This is the case when I look at all geography majors—the whole population. But if I take a sample of geography majors, Michael is not likely to be in the sample. If I take another sample, he is not likely to be in that sample, either. (There are lots of geography majors over the years, and only one Michael Jordan.) If I take the average of each of these samples and plot these on a histogram, I have a distribution of averages. I can do this over and over and over again. Maybe one of these samples will include Michael Jordan and that particular average will be skewed, but otherwise, I have mostly non-skewed averages. The distribution of all these sample averages is normal.

> There is only one Michael Jordan.

It is this phenomenon that allows us to assume normality with almost all applied statistics calculations. So if you are using statistics with a sample and someone questions your work because there are some outliers in the population, you can simply refer to the central limit theorem and say you'll check out the outliers, and watch their eyes glaze over.

> We generally get to assume our data are normally distributed, which makes life *sooo* much easier!

In the next chapter, we'll discuss how the normal curve, standard deviations, and *z*-scores set the stage for inferential statistics, where we are no longer describing a population but trying to infer something about a population from just a sample.
Onward!

"So even though we seem to be far above the average in terms of

our GO debt per capita, we are really not that unusual?" The council member sounded surprised.

"Yes, ma'am. The data are really spread out. In fact, it is only when you look at what the debt is used for that we can get some good comparisons."

"Well, can we do that?"

"I already did. If you look at this next slide, you'll see the ten other states that are using GO debt in the same way that we are. We are right in the middle in terms of our per capita debt levels."

"So do you feel that we can increase our debt without any problem?" asked the chair.

"I didn't say that. That is a different question. I can just say that we are not unusual," Nina said with a slight smile.

Review questions

1. What is a standard deviation, and what is its purpose?

2. If the mean in a data set is higher than the median, what does this indicate about the data?

3. Define central limit theorem. Explain why the mean, median, and mode would be the same value in a normal distribution.

4. What does a z-score represent? If someone told you that a data point in a data set has the z-score of plus 2, what could you assume?

5. Why can we assume that most data sets are normally distributed?

6. How can we use a z-score if the data set is not normally distributed?

7. How might your own local government use a z-score to examine its efficiency or effectiveness?

8. What data would you need for this example?

9. In your example, what z-score would you want the data set representing your community to have?

10. Explain how this could be true: "The distribution of an average tends to be normal, even when the distribution from which the average is computed is not."

How Much Is Not Much?

5

[PROBABILITY]

Chuck was happy. He had already prepared the agenda for Monday night's meeting, which held nothing particularly controversial; the weekend was supposed to be sunny, and his golf clubs were waiting. Only a few hours to go on a beautiful Friday afternoon until five o'clock.

Then he sighed. What an illusion. As city manager, he was never really off the clock. Last weekend it was the grand opening of the new animal shelter. This weekend, although nothing was scheduled, that didn't mean he wouldn't get a call about a spill at the sewage plant or a house with forty pit bulls discovered in it. He chuckled. That had actually happened in the next county, and he and all the other surrounding jurisdictions had to provide space for the pit bulls because the county shelter couldn't handle them all. And there might have been more dogs, but neighbors stopped by and some dogs "disappeared" as soon as the notice started going out on police scanners. What a mess. Oh well, he could at least hope for a calm weekend.

Chuck spent another two hours reviewing the town's personnel policies. If anything was going to be controversial in the coming week, it was going to be whether to expand the volunteer firefighter force or to hire another career firefighter. The phone rang.

"Chuck, did you hear the news about Red Oak?" Red Oak was not the local baseball team; it was a small community to the northeast of Council Top, along the river. The caller was John Vernon, a friend who was a retired firefighter. John listened to the emergency medical services scanner all the time, following what happened where over the whole region.

"No, what's up, John?"

"There's a fire at the old Stanley Furniture store on Route 5 going out of town. It is still burning—probably will for days. The place was packed with furniture that the owners were going to sell at an auction at the end of the month."

"Oh, geez. Sounds like it would take four or five crews."

"There's more: the roof collapsed about a half hour ago, with three guys inside. Two are out, but one is missing."

"Oh, no." Chuck was quiet for a moment.

"Yeah."

"You know this stuff, John. What's the chance he'll be found?"

"After a half hour, not much, based on my experience."

"Red Oak is an all-volunteer force, isn't it?"

"Yep, from what I know, the initial crew response was volunteer. I don't know which other crews from neighboring towns are there now."

"I'd better talk to our fire chief to see about what support efforts are going on. Thanks for letting me know, John."

"Sure, Chuck. I'll talk to you later."

The day didn't seem so sunny anymore. Chuck started making phone calls, wondering what "not much" meant in terms of probability.

The topic that most seems to scare students in public administration research methods is **probability.** But to move from descriptive statistics to inferential statistics, we need to understand probability. More specifically, we need to understand how probability relates to confidence and patterns in the data. Take time with the material below. There are no big formulas and not a lot of numbers, but the concepts are at the heart of the rest of the book.

First a little review. Descriptive statistics simply describe the data we have in hand. We cannot make larger generalizations about the world; we can only describe what is right in front of us. It is what it is. There is no chance involved, no error other than human error in measuring the data or in calculating the descriptive statistic value.

Inferential statistics are different.

Inferential statistics

With inferential statistics we try to infer something about the broader world from a sample of data. For example, we could not know exactly what the average income is in the city of Seattle unless we asked every single person earning a living in the city what his or her income is—and even then, our answer probably would not be accurate because some people would lie. In addition, the value would change the next day, since someone would quit a job, someone else would be hired, someone else would die, and someone else would get a raise.

When you have a relatively small number of data points, or observations, in a population, you can go ahead and gather information for every unit; for example, you could gather data for all fifty states since all fifty states is a population. You might be able to get data on income for a population if all you want to know is the exact average income on your street. It is possible to go to each house and ask. But with most research questions, the population is much larger, and we cannot possibly ask every single person, or survey every single house, or observe every single classroom, or test every single student.

Is the sample a good representation of the population? Ah, Watson, that is the question!

So we take a sample. And we hope that this sample is a good representative of the larger whole. In other words, we hope that from the sample, we can infer something about the larger population. This is where probability comes in. Either it is very likely that the sample is a good representation of the population, or it is not very likely. It is very probable, or it is not very probable. There is a good chance of the sample being representative, or there is not a good chance.

What is the *likelihood*, the *probability*, the *chance* of something happening? I use these terms interchangeably—not to give you a headache but to make you realize that these terms mean the same thing. All three are used commonly in working with data in cities and counties.

Recently, Sean, a former student, told me that certain parts of statistics suddenly "clicked" with him when he realized that it applied to his work in Iraq. He was part of a team in charge of a roadblock in Iraq, and they noticed that when it rained, they discovered much larger caches of weapons in vehicles. The question he asked was, was this random luck at his post, or was it representative of all roadblocks in Iraq? He did not actually do the calculations, but he understood how he could apply statistics to that question. He wanted to know if his sample was representative of the whole population of cars stopped at roadblocks in Iraq. The material in this chapter will help you with this type of question.

More importantly, an understanding of probability will help with another question. Are two things related? In Sean's case, were insurgents trying to pass through more weapons in certain weather conditions? Were rain and weapons transfers related? We can't know that for sure, but we can try to assess how likely it is.

Of course, statistics professors have to make it more complicated. Instead of just checking to see how likely it is that two things are related, we approach the question by asking how likely it is that the two things are *un*related. In other words, how likely is it that one would see the data you have, such as many roadblocks in rainstorms where soldiers find weapons, if there were no relationship? Was it just by chance that, during rainstorms, lots of people who were stopped had weapons?

Anything can be random.

I must stop here and state a fact, a rule, something that—even if it is hard to believe—you must accept as a scientist: *anything* can be random. There is no total, absolute confidence in two things being related. We might be very, very confident— even 99.9999% sure—but there is always a chance that the data we have are the result of random chance. For example, while very, very improbable, you could flip a coin a million times and get "heads" every time. It is *possible.* Just not probable.

This is where the concept of confidence comes in. There is always a very small, tiny, infinitesimal chance that the data you have are not representative of the population, or that two groups of data are not related even when it looks as though they are. If the chance of the data being random is very, very low—say, 5% or lower— you can be pretty confident in saying that the survey data are a *valid* representation of the population (remember that term from earlier in the book?), or that the two groups of data are related. If the chance of the data being random is higher—say, 20% or 30%—you would not be as confident in saying that there is a relationship.

How do we understand whether there is a small chance or a large chance that the data are random? Patterns in the data. Do your data seem unusual given other data, or do they seem to fit? If I wanted to know whether my child's test score shows that he is a genius, I would ask whether it falls within or above the general pattern of the data for most other kids. If his score were high relative to the other kids' scores, I would be very confident in saying that he did really well on the test. If his score were not that different from most other kids' scores, I wouldn't be very confident in my claim of his mental prowess.

In the same vein, if there is a clear, direct pattern in the data, we are more likely to say that there is a relationship between two things. Take weather and weapons, for example: if the number of weapons found always goes up when it rains, I would be pretty confident that there is a relationship between the two. If it only happened sometimes, I would be less confident that there is a relationship between them. Data probability and confidence: these are the cornerstones of statistics. We have already talked about data. We will revisit the ideas of probability and confidence multiple times here and in the coming chapters.

Basic law of probability

There are two important terms to understand when you speak of probability: an event and an outcome. An **event** might be easily described as something that happens that can have multiple outcomes—for example, when a choice is made, something changes, or a separation into different groups takes place. It could be a very small, minute choice, such as deciding what socks to wear on a particular day, or a major happening, such as giving birth to a child. The **outcome** is what results: you wear blue socks, or the new addition to your family is a boy.

The basic law of probability is as follows:

$$\frac{\text{The number of ways that a particular outcome can happen}}{\text{The number of ways that all possible outcomes can happen}} = \text{Probability}$$

In a way, probability is just working with fractions, knowing what goes on top and what goes on the bottom. The best example, and one that is used over and over again, is the infamous coin flip. If you have a coin (assuming it is legitimate and not rigged), and you flip it 100 times, you will get heads about half the time and tails about half the time. Okay, I realize that this statement will prompt some smart aleck out there to actually flip a coin 100 times just to test that statement, and he or she will actually get 54 heads and 46 tails, or 53 heads and 47 tails, or 35 heads and 65 tails. But I assure you, if 100 people flipped the coin, on average, one half of the flips would be heads and one half of the flips would be tails. This is how probabilities are determined. Each flip is an event. There are two possible outcomes. In the long run, if you could flip a coin 100 times over and over and over and over again, millions of times, the number of times that heads would come up is, on average, 50 out of 100 flips.

A probability is just a fraction.

What is the probability of seeing a boy when you first lay eyes on a newborn child? We know, over the long run—over about a couple billion "events" over the course of history—that there is about a 51% chance of having a boy and about a 49% chance of having a girl. (We suspect that since girls are slightly more likely to survive to age one and live longer on average, nature gives boys a fighting chance by giving them the birth edge.)

Both of these examples demonstrate **posterior probabilities**—that is, probabilities that are established after having the event take place over and over again. Basically, we learn probability by experience.

We can figure out probabilities in another way, too. What is the probability of you wearing blue socks tomorrow? Depends on how many blue socks, and socks of other colors, are in your drawer when you are making the decision (the event). **A priori probabilities** is a term used for those probabilities that you know in advance without ever testing the event. If all my socks are blue there is a 100% chance that, if I wear a pair of my socks (the event), the socks will be blue (the outcome). If only one pair of socks is blue and 99 pairs are black, my chance of picking the blue pair is one out of 100, or 1%. If 5 pairs of socks are blue, and the remaining 20 pairs are black, then my chance of picking a blue pair is 5/25, or 1/5, or 20%. Another example: if there are 100 students in a room, 25 of them women and 75 of them men, and I pick one at random (the event), the probability of picking a woman is 25/100 or 1/4, or 25% (the outcome). These are all a priori probabilities.

These probabilities are easy. But life is never easy, and local government management is only slightly less complicated than life. How do we determine more complex probabilities and use them for decision making? We need to use some basic rules to let us learn the language of probabilities.

First, something must happen. That is, if an outcome is possible, there is a probability associated with it. In a simple but happy example, with the event of having a healthy baby there are two possible outcomes: (1) having a new baby boy or (2) having a new baby girl. So if you add up the probability of having a girl and the probability of having a boy, you have all possible outcomes, and 100% of the probability:

Probability of boy + probability of girl = 100%.

This means that if we know the probability of one outcome, we also know the probability that that particular outcome will *not* happen. When there are only two possible outcomes, we know that if one outcome does not occur, the other outcome will. Thus, if I know the probability of having a girl (49%), I don't have to look at the actual data to know that the probability of having a boy (or not a girl) is 100% minus 49%, or 51%. Often, we state only one probability and leave the other unstated, as when we say that there is a 60% chance of rain tomorrow. Of course, that means there is a 40% chance that it will not rain.

> Be specific and careful about what you want to know when working with probabilities: if you ask the wrong question, you will get the wrong answer.

If there are multiple possible outcomes, things get a little more complicated, and we need to be clear about which outcome we are examining. For example, usually one thinks of only two main employee categories in local government: full time and part time. But any good HR manager knows that there are multiple categories. Usually a government would have four different categories: permanent full-time, permanent part-time, temporary full-time, and temporary part-time employees. If I pick an employee at random, there is a probability associated with each category. Added up, the probabilities of all the categories equals 100%:

Probability (permanent full time) + Probability (permanent part time) + Probability (temporary full time) + Probability (temporary part time) = 100%.

In statistics, we often replace the word *probability* with just a *p* and write this idea as

$$p \text{ (permanent full time)} + p \text{ (permanent part time)} \dots \text{and so on.}$$

If we want to pick an employee at random and want to know the chance of getting a particular type of employee, we take the number of employees in that category divided by the number of total employees. If you know the probability of getting an employee in that category, you also know, automatically, the probability of *not* getting an employee in that category—or, in other words, the probability of getting an employee from one of all the other categories.

What often confuses people is this kind of probability—the probability of not one characteristic, but of two or more characteristics that can be combined in different ways. In the probability tree below, we have two different characteristics: (1) whether someone is permanent or temporary, and (2) whether he or she is a full-time or a part-time employee. This gives us a set of options for each of the two characteristics, or four different kinds of outcomes, as you can see in Figure 5–1. Each set of options is considered an event.

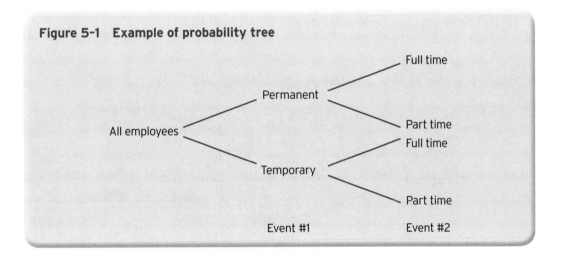

Figure 5-1   Example of probability tree

Let's fill out this probability tree to demonstrate how researchers use probabilities. Say that a local government has 100 employees, 70 of whom are permanent and 30 of whom are temporary. Our chart would begin to look like the probability tree in Figure 5–2.

Figure 5-2   Another example of a probability tree

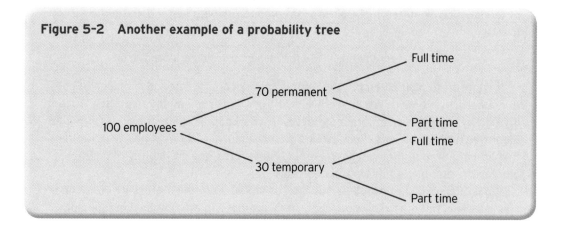

If you picked an employee at random, there is a 70% chance (70/100 or 0.70) that the employee would be permanent. Likewise, there is a 30% chance (30/100 or 0.30) that the employee would be temporary. Now let's add the next event: whether the employees are full time or part time. Of all the permanent employees, 50 work full time and 20 work part time. Of all the temporary employees, 5 are full time and 25 are part time. Let's put those numbers in (see Figure 5–3).

Figure 5-3   Yet another example of a probability tree

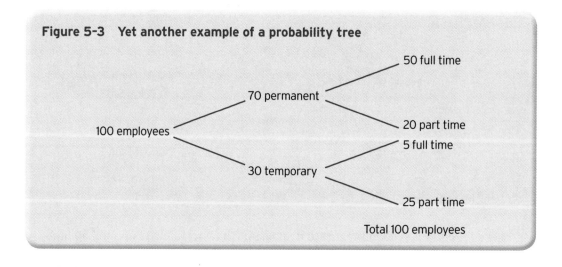

From the numbers that are shown in Figure 5–3, I can calculate a whole variety of probabilities. The key to doing this correctly is to understand exactly what you are measuring. Figure 5–4 shows the tree with probabilities put in for each event in addition to numbers. In each case, we are taking the part over the whole or, in other words, the specific "outcome" over all possible outcomes in that part of the tree.

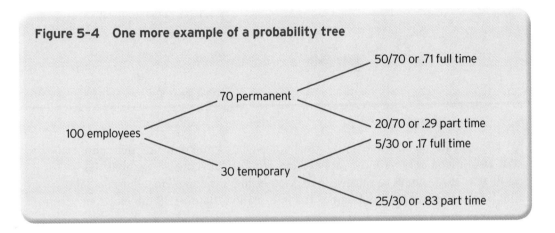

Figure 5-4   One more example of a probability tree

100 employees

70 permanent
- 50/70 or .71 full time
- 20/70 or .29 part time

30 temporary
- 5/30 or .17 full time
- 25/30 or .83 part time

Of all the permanent employees, 71% are full time and 29% are part time. Of all the temporary employees, 17% are full time and 83% are part time. These are conditional probabilities; that is, the probability is an outcome in the second event, given a particular outcome in the first event. In other words we might say, "Given that an employee is permanent, there is about a 70% chance that he or she would be full time," or "Most permanent employees are full time." For these probabilities we are only on the top half of the tree, having followed the path up to permanent employees and, from there, calculated new probabilities for the next event, or branch of the tree. How would you describe the probabilities in the bottom half?

Now, what if I want to know the probability of both events at the same time? That is, out of all the employees, what is the likelihood that I would meet someone who is both permanent *and* full time. For this, I would need to know the number of people in this specific joint category. To find this out, we take the numbers that we show in Figure 5–4, and calculate the probabilities for each end point, which are now displayed in Figure 5–5.

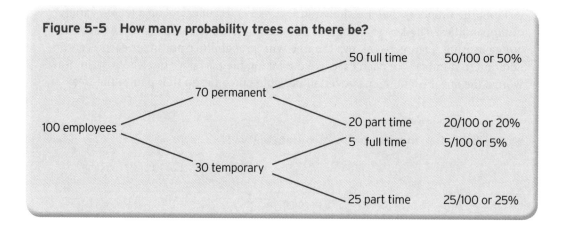

Figure 5-5   How many probability trees can there be?

100 employees
- 70 permanent
  - 50 full time → 50/100 or 50%
  - 20 part time → 20/100 or 20%
- 30 temporary
  - 5 full time → 5/100 or 5%
  - 25 part time → 25/100 or 25%

It is easy to calculate the joint probabilities when you know the final numbers. But what if you only have the probabilities with each event? For example, let's assume that the employee structure in another town is completely different. You don't have the numbers, but here is the information that the HR director sent you in an e-mail:

> We are a beach resort town, so we have a lot more temporary employees than other towns. They make up 80% of our workforce. Of the temporary employees, to keep benefit costs down, about 95% are part time. We don't have any permanent part-time employees. We had to get rid of them in the last round of state budget cuts.

From this information, we can figure out the other percentages for our tree. If 80% of the employees are temporary, then the other 20% must be permanent. If there are no permanent part timers, then 100% of the permanent employees must be full time (see Figure 5–6).

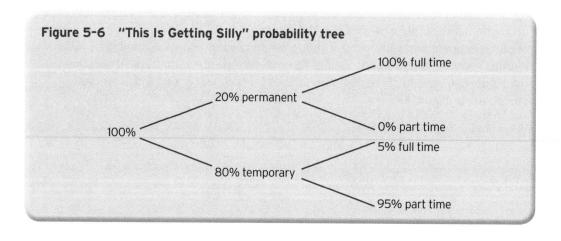

Figure 5-6   "This Is Getting Silly" probability tree

100%
- 20% permanent
  - 100% full time
  - 0% part time
- 80% temporary
  - 5% full time
  - 95% part time

Now we can determine the joint probabilities by multiplying the probabilities in each branch of the tree.

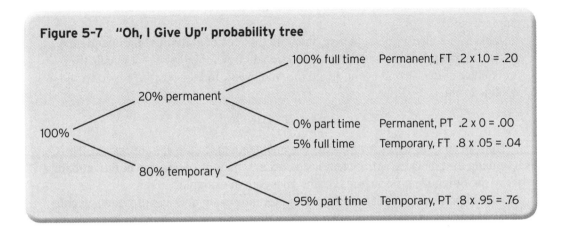

Figure 5-7   "Oh, I Give Up" probability tree

Just as with the number chart, the probabilities total 100%. Another way to present this same information is in a table; using the information from the paragraph above, we can fill in the numbers (see Table 5-1). I just used 100 employees as an example because it matches 100%. But you could follow the information for any number of employees.

Table 5-1   Example of probability chart (thank goodness it's not a tree) using employee type information

	Employee status		
Employee type	Full time	Part time	Total
Permanent	20	0	20
Temporary	4	76	80
Total	24	76	100

From a table like this, you can produce a wide array of probabilities as long as you keep straight what is the base (denominator) of the fraction and what is the portion (numerator) of the fraction—or, in other words, what particular outcome you are interested in over what group of all outcomes. Take the following example of a simple problem that you can solve by using the numbers in Table 5-1:

You are planning the annual employee picnic and want to play a softball game pitting the permanent full-time players against the temporary part-time players. How many people would be left out of the game to serve as umpires? Four—just enough. I got the answer by adding the number of permanent full-time employees (20) to the number of temporary part-time employees (76). This would be compared to the other two entries, temporary full-time employees (4) and permanent part-time employees (0).

Table 5–1 is also a good place to illustrate the idea of **statistical independence.** Statistical independence exists when the probability of the first event equals the probability of the second event, given the first event. In logic symbols, you would see this formula:

$$p(A) = p(A \text{ given } B).$$

Huh? In simpler terms, two events are independent if they are not related. Thus, assuming that they are not related, if one occurs, there is no change in the probability of the other event occurring. Let me give you an example:

I am interviewing candidates for a summer internship and want to hire someone local. My assistant has told me that about half the candidates grew up in the immediate area (probability of being a "local" = 50%). The first candidate is ready to come in. My assistant says, "I think you will like her; she has lots of experience."

Now, does knowing that the person has experience tell you anything about whether that person is a local? Are these two things linked? Does the probability of being a local have any influence on being experienced? To put it in the format of our formula: does the probability of a person being experienced equal the probability of that person being experienced *given that* he or she is a local? I would say no. I would generally say that being a local and being experienced are not linked. They are independent. In other words, I think the probability of being a local = 50%. The probability of being a local, given that one is experienced, is still 50%. Knowing whether someone is experienced does not help you guess whether the person is a local.

Let's run through an example of two probabilities that are *not* independent. Using our previous example of full-time and part-time employees, if I know that the person standing in front of me is full time, would it help me to guess whether he or she is a permanent employee? Let's look at the formula:

Probability (permanent employee) = ? Probability (permanent employee given full time).

From Table 5–1 we know that there are 20 permanent employees out of all 100 employees. This means that the probability of being a permanent employee is 20%. That is the first part of our formula. For the second part of the formula, we need the number of permanent employees out of all full-time employees. The number of all full-time employees is 24. Of those, 20 are permanent. Thus, the probability of being permanent, given that the employee is full time, is 20 over 24, or 83%. Does 20% equal 83%? No! In this case, knowing that someone is full time *does* change the probability that the person is permanent, so we *can* use the information of full-time status to help with our guess about being permanent. The two probabilities—that of being full time and that of being permanent—are not independent. They are dependent.

Another way to see how two events can be dependent is by looking for certain combinations of attributes. For example, to continue with the same example, let's say you need to select a committee of employees. The first person is chosen at random from all employees. What is the likelihood (probability) that the person is a permanent employee? As I said above, it is 20%. What is the likelihood that the second person chosen is a permanent employee? You might guess 20% again, and you would be almost right. But the ratio is a little different. Instead of having 20 permanent employees that could be chosen, there are only 19: remember, we already chose one, so that person is out of the mix now! In addition, our total pool is made up of only 99 employees, instead of 100. So the probability of having a permanent employee is now 19 over 99, or 19%; that's close, but different. When you have a very, very large pool of possible outcomes, a slight change such as pulling one person out doesn't show up in a difference in probabilities. But when the pool is small, the outcome of the first event (such as picking someone for a committee) does have an impact on the second event. Knowing who is chosen first affects my guess for who is chosen second. In the trees shown above, when events are dependent, probabilities for the second event depend on what path is taken in the first event.

Why is the distinction of dependence and independence important? It is a clue about association, which we will discuss in later chapters. If probabilities are dependent, then there is probably going to be an association between the two things, perhaps even a causal relationship. But that is getting ahead of ourselves….

"Hell, Chuck, the death in Red Oak just proves my point. We shouldn't rely on volunteer firefighters to fight fires. They are more likely to die in those buildings." Rex and Will had joined Chuck at the bar after their golf game. Rex ran the local hobby shop, complete with model airplanes, buckets of clay, balsa wood, trading cards, and, recently, Lego sets. For some reason, Lego was the hot new hobby/toy, and he was selling Legos as fast as he could stock them. Wherever Rex was, Will could be found close behind. Will teased Rex about turning his childhood into his job, but he never seemed to be far from Rex's shop—or from the Lego sets.

The topic of conversation wasn't as light as the usual joking. Rex's father was a prominent community member and a strong advocate for increasing the professional firefighter force. Rex had been convinced that this was the right choice to make and was pressing his point with Chuck.

"I don't know, Rex. I just don't know what to do. Everyone at the meeting on Monday is going to be focused on whether adding more volunteers to the fire squad is a good idea. Instead of us looking at the facts and trying to make the best decision, it is going to be very emotional," said Chuck. "I just don't want to get carried away with a lot of assumptions and make a bad decision."

"Well, you know what they say about assumptions: they make an ass out of u and…," started Will, before Rex threw a pretzel at him. "Seriously, why not get the numbers before the meeting?"

"What do you mean?"

"Instead of letting people just assume volunteers are more at risk in fires, why not find out some facts. If a firefighter dies in fighting a fire, is she or he more likely to be a volunteer or a professional?"

"It has got to be volunteer. C'mon, Will, don't you think the professionals know better what they are doing?"

"I'm not saying anything about anybody. I just want to know what the numbers actually are!"

Chuck just sat and chewed on his pretzel. "I have to stop by the office for a sec before we go get pizza, guys. See you at the Pizza Palace in about 45 minutes? Might as well order a pitcher of pop this time instead of individual glasses, as long as we're all ordering Diet Coke."

Rex looked down at his no-longer-slim-and-trim belly. "Yeah, I guess so."

Review questions

1. What are the differences between inferential statistics and probability? How are they similar?

2. How do random data relate to the confidence level? In other words, if the chance that data are random is very low, how does that affect the confidence level?

3. What is an event? Give an example.

4. What is an outcome? Give an example.

5. What is the law of probability? Give an example.

6. What is a probability tree? Make a tree with 100 employees: 65 permanent, 35 temporary, 50 full time, and 50 part time.

7. What are conditional probabilities? From the example above, what would be the conditional probabilities?

8. Look at the two problems described at the end of the chapter (hiring the summer intern and guessing whether the full-time employee is permanent or temporary). How would you use either the probability tree or the table to solve the problems?

9. Create a probability tree of your own.

10. Use that probability tree to create a table.

That Picture Doesn't Look a Thing Like Me!

[SAMPLES VERSUS POPULATIONS]

Chuck sat down with his buddies. The pitcher of Diet Coke was already half gone. But Chuck knew he had timed it just right: there was no pizza yet, but it must be on its way any minute. "OK, guys, I set our new analyst on this, and she was able to find me the numbers in about two minutes, as usual."

"What do you mean?" asked Rex.

"You always show up right when the pizza is coming to the table–how do you do that?" joked Will. The waitress placed the supreme pizza (minus olives) on the table and distributed the plates and napkins. "Anyone need forks?"

The three guys shook their heads no.

"Nina was able to get the numbers–whether a volunteer firefighter is more likely to die in the course of fighting a fire than a professional firefighter."

"Well, thanks for lightening up the conversation, Chuck!" said Rex.

"Come on, guys. You know that I am going to be grilled on this tomorrow night at the council meeting. So I better figure it out now. Look at this table." He placed a copy of the table (shown here on page 76) before each of the men.

"Nationwide, out of the 85 firefighter deaths in 2008, volunteers did account for a higher percentage. But here's what is really interesting. Of all the professionals' deaths, almost half occurred at the fire ground; of all the volunteer deaths, however, only 21% occurred at the fire ground while almost half occurred while the volunteers were responding to or returning from an alarm!" Chuck pointed at the numbers for emphasis.

"So if you are a volunteer, you're about twice as likely to die in a car crash on the way to the fire than to die at the fire?" Rex was very interested in the paper, drawing it close to his chair.

Table 6-1   **Comparison of on-duty deaths between career and volunteer firefighters, 2008**

Type of duty	Career firefighters		Volunteer firefighters	
	No.	%	No.	%
Responding to or returning from alarm	1	4	26	45
Operating at fire ground	12	44	12	21
Operating at nonfire emergencies	3	11	8	14
Training	2	7	5	9
Other on-duty	9	33	7	12
Total	27	100	58	100

Source: Reproduced with permission from Rita F. Fahy, Paul R. LeBlanc, and Joseph L. Molis, *Firefighter Fatalities in the United States–2008* (Quincy, Mass.: Fire Analysis and Research Division, National Fire Protection Association, copyright © 2009), 16.

Note: Percentages do not total 100% because of rounding.

"Yup," Chuck nodded.

"Wow. Volunteers are over 10 times as likely to die going to or coming from the fire than professionals?"

"Yup."

"What are you guys talking about?" asked Will. His attention had been on the pizza.

"Twenty-one percent of volunteer deaths were at the fire ground, compared to 44% of professional firefighter deaths. That is where we get the 'about twice as likely' figure. And 45% of volunteer deaths were in car crashes (presumably, if they were traveling to or from the fire), but those accounted for only 4% of professional firefighter deaths. Forty-five is 11 times higher than 4. It's just a different way to say the same thing, but the comparisons are more impressive. Rex likes to be impressive," said Chuck with a smile. He reached for the biggest piece of pizza, wrapping up the dripping, stretching cheese over the top as he pulled it off the pan.

"Ok, you have convinced me. Volunteers are not more likely to die in fighting a fire itself. So you can't use that argument to push for hiring only professionals. But you could use these numbers to argue that volunteers need some better way to get to a fire other than screaming down the road with just their regular car flashers going," said Will.

"What do our guys do, Chuck?" asked Rex. "Do they go straight to the fire, or do they report to the station and then use a fire station vehicle?"

"I'm not sure, but now I am really curious. I'm also curious about the location of our fires—you know, if they are more rural than in town, that kind of thing. Also, just because these are national figures doesn't mean they hold for us. We might have a much better safety record."

"Oh, yeah, Chuck, Stan and his boys are real safe drivers!" Everyone laughed. Stan was a prominent volunteer firefighter and had the newest F110 pickup in town. He loved showing how much power it had, and if asked about safe drivers, Stan's name would not necessarily be the first to jump to mind.

Rex took another look at the sheet. "Are these all the deaths, or just a sample?"

"Huh?" Chuck almost choked on his slice. "You're starting to talk like Nina!"

"It looks like these are all the deaths in 2008. It is a population. A sample is a smaller group, a subgroup you might say, that represents the larger population. But I don't think it matters; I think we are looking at the wrong thing. Wouldn't it be better to look at injuries? They would be a lot more common and might give you a different picture. Of course, it would be pretty impossible to get a full population of injury data for the country. And like you said, national figures lump everything together—cities, counties, big, small. I might just look at some injury figures for similar-sized towns in the Midwest—not all, though, because that would be too much work, even if you could get the data. Just a sample."

"Now I *know* you are talking like Nina!"

If you wanted to know what people thought about a presidential candidate before an election, it would be impossible to interview everyone in the country. You would have to interview just some of the people and hope these folks' views reflected general national opinion. This process—hoping the opinion or behavior of a subgroup is representative of the larger group—is called **sampling.**

Drawing conclusions (inferences) from samples

Almost all research is based on samples. Samples allow us to take a small number of observations and make inferences about the larger population. Samples give us an estimate of what the value in question is. For example, say a local government wants to know the citizens' opinions about a new public swimming pool. It could try to telephone everyone in town, but, of course, that is much too expensive and practically impossible. Therefore, instead of knowing the *real* average opinion by talking to everyone in town, the local government has to rely instead on an *estimate*.

Any estimate is going to include some error, so how do we know if our estimate is a good one? This is really the question people ask when they say, "Is it a good sample?" A good sample should result in a good estimate most of the time. But no matter how hard we try, we will always have some error in our sample. How do we get a sense of how much error there is?

Analysts do this with a number called the **standard error,** which works in a similar way as the standard deviation. If we were to take multiple samples—say, 100 samples from a population—and graph all of their means, we would have a histogram. Draw a line over that histogram, and we have a curve. We know from the central limit theorem that the curve is going to be a normal curve. Is that curve spread out, which would tell us that the averages in our samples are all over the place? That is, do the averages in our samples have a wide distribution, as shown in Figure 6–1, or a narrow distribution, as shown in Figure 6–2? If our curve looks like Figure 6–1, our samples have a lot of error. If in one case, the sample average is over here, while in another case, the sample average is over there, it would be hard to trust any particular sample, especially if it is small.

Figure 6-1   Sample with lots of variation (and thus lots of error)

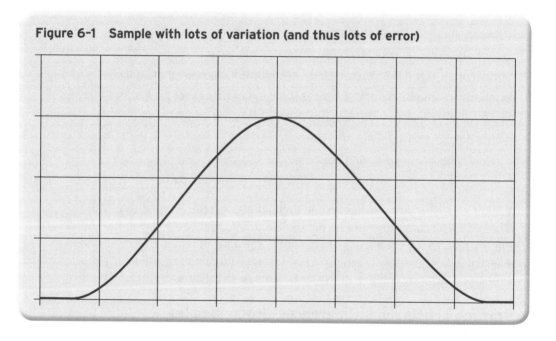

The formula for sample error is

$$\text{Sample error} = \frac{\text{Standard deviation for sampling population}}{\text{Square root of sample size}}.$$

Figure 6-2   Sample with less variation (and thus less error)

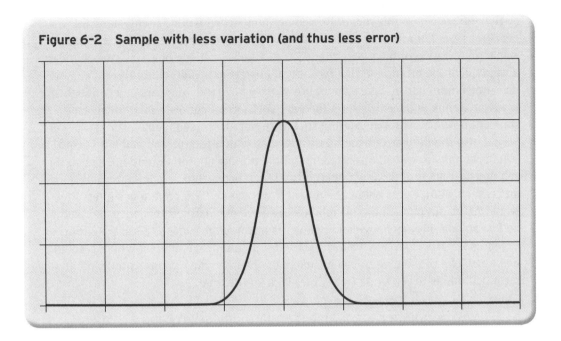

Remember, the standard error is the estimate of how much error we have when sampling. Don't worry too much about the formula because, as with standard deviation, most spreadsheet programs will calculate it for you.

Now, when we looked at a population with a normal distribution and we found out what the standard deviation was, we could use the z-score to tell us what percentage of values fell between two numbers, or what percentage of the values in the population was above or below any particular number. In the same way, we can use the standard error to give us a range within which we hope the true mean falls. This range, which is on either side of the sample mean, is called the **confidence interval.** We usually believe that the true mean falls somewhere within this range. In Figure 6–3, the sample mean is 50, but the confidence interval is plus or minus 3. In other words, while our estimate of the mean is 50, we are saying that we hope and expect the true mean to really be somewhere between 47 and 53.

Figure 6-3   Estimate with confidence interval

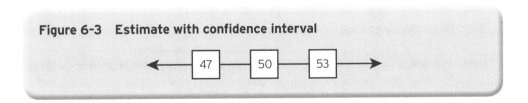

How do we set up this range? Remember how, when working with standard deviations, we knew that in normal curves, 68% of all observations fall within one standard deviation of the mean, that 95% of all observations lie within two standard deviations of the mean, and that 99% of all observations fall within three standard deviations of the mean? The same ratios work with standard errors and confidence intervals (thank you, central limit theorem and normal curves!). Just as we used standard deviations as a measuring stick with population data and called it a *z*-score, we can use standard error as a measuring stick with a sample and call it a **t-score.** With a sample of over 30 observations (not a number chosen at random, as you'll see shortly!), 95% of those observations will fall between two standard errors above and two standard errors below the mean. If we want a 95% confidence interval, we would figure out our sample mean and count two standard errors above and below it. Two standard errors above and below the mean is the same as a *t*-score of plus or minus 2. These two new values bookend our confidence interval with a high end and a low end of the range. This means that, given the data in our sample, the true mean will fall between these two values 95% of the time.

> With populations, you use standard deviations and *z*-scores. With samples, you use standard errors and *t*-scores. Either way, you are usually looking for a score of 2 to say that something interesting is going on.

The standard error is even more useful than that. Remember how we could find any point from a population mean and understand how far away it was from that mean by measuring the distance in terms of standard deviations? This allowed us to understand whether the observation in front of us was dramatically different from the rest of the data. If an observation was more than two standard deviations above or below the mean, it was located in the tails of the distribution of the population—a point very different from the average.

The same logic goes for samples, but instead of using standard deviations and *z*-scores, we use standard errors and *t*-scores. The formula for a *t*-score is

$$\frac{\text{Sample mean – the population mean}}{\text{Standard error}}.$$

What this formula basically says is that if the sample mean is really far away from the true mean, the sample is really different from the population.

Now sometimes we don't have the true mean; we just have a comparison point, such as the mean from the population of data from last year, or the mean from the population of data from another local government, or what we think the true mean is. The mechanics are the same. We are measuring the distance between two points, and our measuring stick is the standard error in our reference sample.

And this is where the sample size of 30 is important. Remember how we discussed that most data we encounter will either have a normal distribution, more or less, or can be assumed to have a normal distribution? That is true in samples above 30 observations. Up to 30, the curve is not exactly normal: it tends to be flatter, and the percentages under it at one or two standard deviations do not stay the same when the number in the sample changes. It is not something that will dramatically affect your calculation, but it will cause your computer program to ask you for the sample size. If your sample is under 30, the computer will make the appropriate adjustment to the values for the confidence interval. Under 30, *t*-scores are slightly different than *z*-scores. Above 30, *z*-scores and *t*-scores mirror each other exactly in terms of the percentage of observations under the curve at any particular point.

Most analysts working with samples want to have a much larger sample size anyway, so the constraint of 30 observations is not that meaningful. Most textbooks on statistics will include a full *z*-score table and a full *t*-score table, showing the percentage under the curve at each value of a *z*-score or *t*-score so that you can look up the associated *z*- or *t*-score for each point. I don't present these tables here because most data analysis programs will do the calculation for you. But you should recognize that with a population of data, any point in the distribution can be measured in standard deviations and *z*-scores; with a sample of data, any point in the distribution can be measured in standard errors and *t*-scores.

We also can compare two samples and ask if they are really from the same population. If you laid the samples on top of each other, it would it look like Figure 6–4:

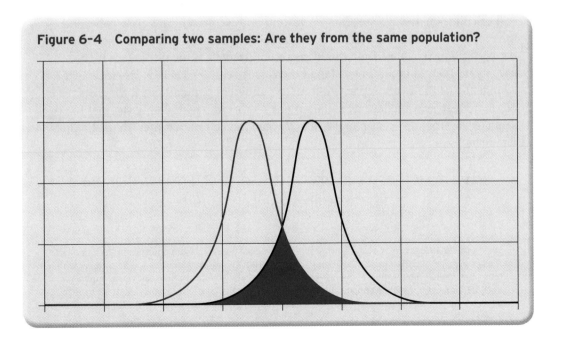

Figure 6-4 Comparing two samples: Are they from the same population?

Or like Figure 6–5:

Figure 6-5   Comparing two samples again: Are they from the same population?

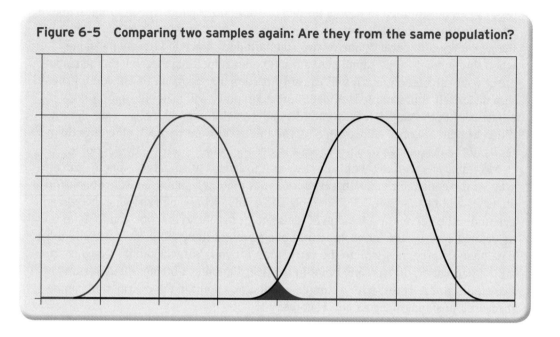

The math is slightly different here because instead of one standard error from one sample, we have two standard errors from two samples. In this case, the computer will calculate an average standard error from both samples.[1] The math is beyond the scope of this text (although it is not difficult). Suffice it to say that the distance between the two values is measured, again, in t-scores. If the distance is high—say, above 1.96, or around two standard errors (t-score = 1.96, or 2)—we are 95% confident that the two samples are from two different populations. If the distance is not that great—say, under one standard error—we can't confidently say that the two samples are from different populations. We can't even say that they are really that different.

> Remember the rule of thumb: A t-score of 2 means that there is a statistically significant difference!

---

1 Your software program may ask you what type of variance you are assuming exists in the samples. Always assume that the samples have unequal variances. This is the highest standard to meet with tests of statistical significance. If the difference is statistically significant between two groups with unequal variances, it will be statistically significant in all other cases. This way, you don't have to worry about whether your assumption is correct; you just automatically choose the toughest standard to beat.

Let's stop here and run through an example. Let's say that a department has insti-tuted a new scheduling program to reduce overtime hours. It's a large department, like a county social services department in an urban area. Because the department records are not fully automated yet, it would be too time-consuming and difficult to gather all the HR data for every employee. Instead, it is much more reasonable to take a sample of employees—say, 100—and look at the average number of overtime hours per person. To what would we compare it? Luckily, we do have all the infor-mation for all employees from the previous year, so we are comparing a sample to a population. Here are the data from our sample:

Sample mean: 7.5
Population mean (taken from previous research): 6.5
Standard error: 0.5
(7.5 – 6.5) / 0.5 = 2
The *t*-score is 2. What can we say?

Confidence levels

We've talked about the confidence interval: the two values above and below our sample mean between which we hope the true mean falls. Now we need to talk about a different use of the word *confidence:* **confidence levels.** Like confidence in-tervals, confidence levels have to do with how good our sample is. With confidence levels, though, we are focused on our conclusion. It is similar to the idea behind a confidence interval but is used in a different way. With a sample, we usually want to know how close our sample mean is to the true mean. That is, is our estimate a good one?

Another way to say this is, "How sure are we that our sample mean is close to the true mean?" Okay, okay, that probably sounds way too geeky. So let's simplify it a bit. How about, "How confident are we that we have a good sample?"

Yes, confidence is a sense of surety, a sense of being right, of doing something well. In statistics, however, confidence has a very specific meaning, and it is related to the idea of probabilities. What is the probability that one might encounter certain data if the conclusion that is based on that data is wrong? This is awkward wording, but true. An example will help. If you wanted to know the average income for the city of Seattle and could interview everyone in the city, you would be able to calcu-late the *exact* average income. Because it is a population, you would be *certain* about the average income you calculate. There is no chance that you could be wrong, absent human error in recording the data or in doing the math.

In a survey, though, there is always a chance that our sample, for some reason, does not accurately reflect average income in Seattle (and here we come back to the idea of sample error). Maybe Bill Gates randomly appeared in our sample and skewed the average to the right or, in other words, pushed the sample average up. Maybe our surveyors decided just to interview people in a very poor part of town, and as a result, the sample average is too low. Or maybe, just by chance, our surveyors only encountered "outliers" who didn't really reflect a representative sample of Seattle citizens.

As we discussed before, with a sample, we can never be 100% confident that our estimate perfectly matches reality. So, as analysts, we are left with deciding how confident we want to be in our conclusions. Analysts normally choose one of three levels of confidence:

- Ninety percent confident. If you choose this confidence level, you are allowing yourself a 10% chance that the conclusions drawn from your data could be wrong. That is, you agree to the standard that 1 out of 10 times, you might draw the wrong conclusion from your data. This probability of being "wrong" is called the **p value.** Officially, the *p* value is the chance of obtaining a result at least as extreme as the one that was actually observed, assuming there is no relationship. The 90% confidence level is associated with a *p* value of .10. (Makes sense, right? If you want to be 90% sure that you have the right answer, you accept a 10% chance of being wrong, thereby covering 100% of all possibilities.)

- Ninety-five percent confident. If you choose this confidence level, you are allowing yourself a 5% chance that the conclusions drawn from your data could be wrong. That is, you agree to the standard that 1 out of 20 times, you might draw the wrong conclusion from the data. The probability of being wrong is only 5%, or a *p* value of .05.

- Ninety-nine percent confident. If you choose this confidence level, you are allowing yourself only a 1% chance that the conclusions drawn from your data could be wrong. That is, you agree to the standard that only 1 out of 100 times, you might draw the wrong conclusion from the data. The probability of being wrong is only 1%, or a *p* value of .01.

Statistics is all about confidence!

Research with very high stakes—such as testing a vaccine for pandemic flu where up to 50% of the population may receive the medicine, or testing an antibiotic for newborn babies where a mistake could mean death—may even warrant a 99.99% confidence level as a standard; that is, you want to very, very certain of your conclusions, with a chance of only 1 out of 10,000 times that you will be wrong. In these cases, you want to allow a *p* value of only .0001, or a .01% chance of being wrong.

To summarize, for every confidence level, there is an associated *p* value. For every *p* value, there is an associated *t*-score. In Table 6–2, we bring confidence levels, *p* values, and *t*-scores together. To reach a higher confidence level, you must reach a lower *p* value (or likelihood that you will reach a wrong conclusion). Reaching this standard means that you need to show a large difference between the two things being compared (sample and population, two samples, etc.). This large difference is

Table 6-2 Confidence levels and associated *p* values and *t*-scores.

Confidence level, %	*p* value	*t*-score
90	.10	1.64
95	.05	1.96
		(or 2, as a rule of thumb)
99	.01	2.58

measured in *t*-scores. The higher the *t*, the lower the *p*. The lower the *p*, the more confident you can be that there is a difference between the two measurements.

The beauty of computers comes through when we realize that they do the work for us! As a consumer of statistical information, I believe that none of the individual calculations is as important as understanding how to interpret the findings. Most of you will have someone else do your actual analysis, but you must be able to understand it and interpret it for the public or elected officials or department managers. For you, I hope this chapter prompts you to ask the following questions when comparing two processes or practices:

• Was there a difference?

• Is that difference statistically significant?

• How confident can we be in that conclusion?

You might notice that I have not used the term *hypothesis* a lot. That is because, outside of dissertations and class presentations (and notwithstanding our discussion in Chapter 1), most public administrators don't use that term. Officially, a hypothesis is a suggested explanation for an observable phenomenon or for a reasoned proposal predicting a possible causal correlation among multiple phenomena. Huh? I usually describe it as a guess—a guess that something is different from something else (and if it is, why? or if it is not, why not?) or that there is a relationship between two things, that something is going on. The term *null hypothesis* denotes the opposite: that there is *not* a difference between two things, that there is no relationship between them, that nothing is going on. The formal terms may be technical for everyday use in government. That is why, in this book, I focus instead on the idea of asking whether there is a difference between two things because that is how we actually use hypotheses every day in public administration. We have not been using the term, but inferential statistics is really about hypothesis testing. We are asking, is there a difference or is something going on (is the hypothesis supported by the data)? Or is there not really a difference or is nothing going on (is the null hypothesis supported by the data)?

You may encounter two other statistical terms related to confidence levels and statistical significance that are hard to remember and use every day, but whose meanings are important: **Type I** and **Type II error.** As we've talked about in this chapter, when you draw a conclusion that is based on data, you have to decide on a level of confidence. How high is the evidence bar going to be before you accept a conclusion? Many would argue that the bar should be as high as possible to ensure that we are drawing the correct conclusion. We all want to be right, right? However, when the bar is set very high, there is always a chance that we may fail to acknowledge a real difference or a real relationship. On the other hand, if we set the bar too low, there is a chance that we will jump to an incorrect conclusion. Damned if you do, damned if you don't. Type I error occurs when you set the bar too low. Type II error occurs when you set the bar too high. If you try to minimize Type I error, you increase the chance that you will commit Type II error. If you try to minimize Type II error, you increase the chance that you will commit Type I error. There is no appropriate confidence level to use for all questions. There is no appropriate level of statistical significance that will be acceptable to everyone. The standard you use, 90% confidence or 99.99% confidence, should be appropriate for the question at hand, and of course, that is a subjective call.

Does the difference really matter? This is called material significance.

There is one more very important question. Statisticians always focus on **statistical significance.** Is the *t*-score high enough? Can we say with confidence that there is a difference between two samples or groups? Can we say that there was a statistically significant change from last year to this year? This is the problem with statisticians: sometimes we are so focused on statistical significance that we miss the follow-on point. Yes, there may be a difference, but *does it really matter?* This is called **material significance.**

Statistical significance is important when you want to say whether there is a difference. Nevertheless, analysts must use their own judgment as to whether the difference is enough to make or change policy—that is, whether it has material significance. I can probably prove that a change in a process, such as an accounting system, would save $100 over a year. The question is, is that a large enough amount of money to warrant making the change? In some cases, decisions are made not on the basis of data, but on the basis of politics, equity, compensation, the law, or community values. Don't waste time on the analysis described here if finding statistical significance will not have an impact on your decision—that is, if the decision is not really about the data. And even if the decision depends on the data, be wary of analysis that describes only statistical significance.

The pizza was gone. The guys had splurged on the second pitcher and gotten regular Coke. The Pizza Palace was slowing down, with only one large family still in the adjoining room. The kids were running around in the back poolroom, pretending to play the working and broken video games; the moms had run out of quarters at least a half hour ago.

"Thanks for the pizza, guys. See you next week," said Chuck.

"Not if we see you first!" replied Rex. Chuck expected that reply. It was the running joke of the last six months. He hoped the group would come up with a new one . . . soon.

"Hey, you almost forgot! Pitch in, buddy!" Will said. This was another of the guys' running jokes: to make a half-hearted effort to see if one of them could slip out without paying. It was a golden rule that each paid an equal share so that they never got into an argument over who would pick up the bill.

Outside, the evening had turned soft, with the sun just down but darkness still a little way off. The crickets and cicadas had started up in earnest, and the frogs in the ditches joined in. Council Top was quiet. There were not even any teenage cruisers out yet. It was hard to think about fires, firefighters, statistics, and death.

Coming up from behind, Rex broke into Chuck's thoughts. "Are you really going to try to get some data on the firefighter issue?"

"Yeah. I would really like to know if there is a difference between how volunteer and professional firefighters do. Not in terms of the quality of their work—I know they bust their butts all the time, and goodness knows they put in enough time—but I wonder if volunteers are injured more than professionals, and if so, whether we could do something about it. It just seems fair."

"Not to mention the insurance money the city would save?" Will said.

"Oh, of course. The better our record, the better the rates. But you know it's more than that," said Chuck.

"I know, I know," Rex said softly. "I feel bad for the folks in Red Oak, too. It is hard for a small town to lose a firefighter. You know, the council might not tell you, but folks think you are a great city manager, Chuck. Don't worry about it too much. See you at the course on Saturday. Same time. And if you want to see the new ripsaw I got, stop by the garage some day after work."

"See you!" said Will, walking across the gravel parking lot. The last family was finally leaving the Pizza Palace, and the lighted sign above the parking lot had been turned off.

"Not if I see you first!" laughed Chuck.

Review questions

1. What is a *t*-score and how does it differ from a *z*-score?

2. Describe the concept of a confidence interval and how you would use it with data.

3. If the distribution in our sample is small and narrow, what does this suggest about our standard error?

4. Define the *p* value and describe a circumstance in which it would be useful.

5. If our data have a *p* value of .05, what does this mean? What is our corresponding confidence level?

6. What is the difference between confidence intervals and confidence levels?

7. In a study with very high stakes, such as testing a new medication to be used with cancer patients, what would you want your confidence level to be? Why? What would be your corresponding *t*-score and *p* value?

8. Write a sample hypothesis. Write the corresponding null hypothesis.

9. Define Type I and Type II errors and explain how they affect research.

10. What is the difference between material significance and statistical significance? Is one more important than the other? Give an example of a situation where you might find statistical significance but not material significance.

The Poll Numbers Are In, and in the Lead Is....

[TAKING A SAMPLE]

Chuck had asked the city council to put off the vote on the firefighter position for two months. He argued that he wanted to reconsider staffing in the entire department—that the department had grown slowly over the years, with someone added full time here and someone else added part time there, but that no one had looked at the current structure for over a decade. "We don't know if the department is right for our city for the next 10 years. This is an opportunity to take a step back and consider if we grew in the right way for our current needs. I hate to just keep adding to the department incrementally. I want to be deliberative about what we do, in line with a department plan."

"Do you think we need a strategic plan for the department?" asked the chair. The public works department had taken on a strategic planning effort three years ago, and its success inside the department and its improved relationship with other departments had encouraged the council to ask about planning in other departments at any opportunity.

"No, maybe not a strategic plan exactly," Chuck said slowly, "but more information about adding just one position. I would like to involve the firefighters more, and perhaps gather some comparison survey data from similar jurisdictions on injury rates for volunteer versus professional firefighters. If there is a difference, a material difference, I would like to know why and see if we can do anything to change it. I would also like to survey the firefighters, both volunteer and professional, about their satisfaction with their work."

Like all good local government managers, Chuck was careful about his public safety workers. The firefighters, police officers, and emergency medical service personnel were the most popular folks in town. They visited the school, hosted pancake break-fasts, and, once a year during the city's annual harvest festival, let the kids ride slowly around town on the fire engine with sirens blaring.

"Are you talking about a study for which we'd have to hire a consultant?" Council-woman Whisnant was always careful about money, and she hated consultants.

"No, I think we can do a solid analysis with Nina. She has experience with these kinds of surveys and knows how to get a good sample."

"Will you get good enough information from a survey? Seems to me you want to talk to everyone, don't you? Would a sample really tell you what you want to know? Don't you need to talk to a whole bunch of people to get good information?" Whisnant was skeptical about everything. It was amazing she ever voted yes on any proposal. That was probably why she had been reelected so many times.

Nina stood up. "Actually, we can talk to a sample of the employees and get fairly solid results, Councilwoman Whisnant. But I will make sure that we apply the highest reasonable standards to the analysis so that we are very confident in our findings."

That sounded just professional enough to impress the councilwoman without making her feel, well, dumb. Nina had already impressed her with an analysis of room occupancy taxes on the hotels in town. If Nina said that she could do it, Whis-nant believed her.

"Well, I don't like waiting, but I agree that we could use more information. And I certainly believe that we should not add permanent employees unless we really need them, even if it is for the fire department," closed Whisnant defiantly. The council ap-proved the delay.

"Are you sure about the sampling question?" Chuck asked Nina as they left the council chambers.

"Sure. No problem. Samples are actually very accurate, if done right."

"Well, do it right, then!" said Chuck as he went into his office.

"Yes, sir!" said Nina, with a mock salute. She set about figuring out exactly what she was going to need to do in two months. Six weeks, actually, given that anything she found would need to be reviewed by multiple sets of eyes in the two weeks before the council considered the findings.

One of the most common questions I receive from local government officials is about sampling. A local government would like to conduct a citizen survey and wonders how many people it needs to contact. Or a manager wants to survey employees about a new HR policy and wonders how to get a good sample and what is a sufficient response rate. This section will go over the most important aspects of sampling.

What is a good sample?

Most people think that samples are simply a small portion of the whole population. Remember, a population is all units of what you are studying, such as all the people in a city, all the students in a school district, or all the states in the country. A sample is a portion of the population, so in that sense, most people are right. However, most people also think that a sample needs to be some set proportion of the population, such as 10% or 20%. Not true! The actual number included in a sample is usually much, much smaller, and it is not a set proportion. However, that small number still can be very, very accurate. Let me explain.

Let's say a city wants to survey citizens about a proposal for a new year-round pool. It wants to use good survey methodology and an adequate sample size to have as good an estimate as possible. The city manager does not want the results to be open to challenge by the local Pool Party Poopers opposition group. The city has 56,000 citizens. The manager, having never read this book, jumps to the conclusion that we would probably need at least 5,000 people in the survey—around 10%—and, therefore, it would cost too much.

> The right sample size depends on three things: precision, confidence, and the spread of the data.

She would be wrong. There is not a "fixed proportion" rule to follow. A good sample size depends on three main things, two of which are determined subjectively by the person doing the sampling: precision, confidence, and the spread of the data. You can think of these things as three different limits, or frames, for the sample.

Frame #1: How precise do you want the estimate to be?

In other words, what is an acceptable **margin of error?** This is entirely up to the person doing the survey. Any *estimate,* a single point, is never going to be absolutely, totally, completely accurate. The estimated average you obtain from your sample will never exactly match the true average. Researchers must accept the fact that they will not find the true value of what they are seeking—whether it's the true average income, the true average height or weight, or the true average opinion. Therefore, a researcher must set the boundaries of what level of "sloppiness" is acceptable when obtaining an estimate.

You hope that your estimate, the single value, is close to the single true value. How close? If you drew a frame around the estimate, hoping to capture the true value in that frame, above or below the value of the estimate, you would draw the frame close around the estimate if you wanted to be very precise. If you want to give yourself lots of room above and below your estimated value, you would allow yourself a larger margin of error—a much larger frame—around your estimate.

The larger the acceptable margin of error, the smaller the sample can be. The smaller the acceptable margin of error, the larger the sample needs to be. This is logical. If you want a more precise estimate and you are not going to give yourself a lot of wiggle room, you will need more information. More information means more observations in your sample.

The level of **precision** you want, or the margin of error that is acceptable, is expressed in terms of what is being measured. If you are measuring income, for example, your margin of error needs to be expressed in terms of dollars. Do you want to come up with an estimate of average income? If so, do you want your acceptable limit, or frame around your estimate, to be plus or minus $1,000? Or do you want your frame to be $5,000 around your estimate? If the former, you would take your sample, calculate the average, and then say, "According to this sample, average income is x, plus or minus $1,000." In other words we estimate that the true value is somewhere in that range. If we use the larger frame, we would say, "According to this sample, average income is x, plus or minus $5,000."

Obviously, the first is better from the point of view of the person using the data because he or she wants the estimate to be as focused, as precise, as possible. But from the researcher's point of view, it is much harder because we have to get a larger sample. From a user's point of view, the larger frame seems sloppy and much too broad. But from a researcher's point of view, it is much easier since it allows for more flexibility and a smaller sample. This tug of war is unavoidable. In most circumstances, you can't have both a small sample and high precision with your estimate.

> If you insist on a very precise estimate, you will need a very large sample. You can't get around it.

Another common way to measure margin of error is in percentages. If you want to survey your local government's population to get an estimate of the proportion of people who own dogs, you will be looking for an estimate measured in percentages. For example, is the population of dog owners only 10% of the population or is it 35%? This could make a big difference to you if you are considering recommending a new leash law! In this case, you must decide if you want an estimate that allows for a 1-percentage-point margin of error, a 3–percentage-point margin of error, or 5-percentage-point margin of error. Just as with dollars, the more precise you wish your estimate to be, the larger your sample will likely need to be.

Frame #2: How confident do you want to be in your results?

In the previous chapter, we introduced the idea of confidence. We talked about three levels of confidence that are commonly used: 90%, 95%, and 99%. If you want to be conservative and only accept conclusions that are very, very likely to be accurate, then you would only accept results that meet the threshold of a 99% confidence level. If you are not as strict and, given the question at hand, are willing to set the bar a little lower as long as you still get results that are very likely to be accurate, then you would use a 90% confidence level.

Remember that confidence is different than precision! You might be okay with a loose level of precision and therefore a larger margin of error, but you want to be 99.99% sure that you are drawing the right conclusion from your data. You may also want a very precise estimate but are comfortable with a 95% confidence level. The two things are different. Combined, they can have a major impact on your prospective sample size. Think about it. If you tolerate only a very small margin of error and want to be 99.99% confident in your results, then both choices need more information and thus a large sample. If you are willing to have a pretty sloppy estimate and only need to be 90% confident in your results, then you can settle for a smaller necessary sample.

Now how does this reasoning fit into determining our sample? *Just like with our margin of error, our choice of confidence level will determine whether we need a large sample or can get by with a smaller sample.* It makes sense: if we want to be very sure about our conclusions, say 99% sure, then we will want more information—and thus a larger sample size. If being 90% confident is sufficient for the task at hand, then we can get by with a smaller sample size. Generally, analysts go for the middle on both. They rely on a moderate margin of error—say, 2 or 3 percentage points—and a 95% confidence level.

Frame #3: How spread out are your data?

The one thing in determining sample size that does not depend on your preference is the spread of your data. Again, once you think about it, it is logical. If everyone in the whole city of Pittsburgh were 5'7" tall, you would not need a large sample to come up with an estimate of Pittsburghers' average height: 5'7". If you measured ten people for your sample, the average would be 5'7". If you added ten more people, the average would still be 5'7".

Let's expand the range of height of the Pittsburghers a little and say that the whole city is between 5'5" and 5'9" tall, in a normal distribution. Let's pretend that the true estimate is still 5'7". You could measure ten people, and the sample estimate may be just a little off—say, 5'6". If you added ten people, your estimate would move—but only slightly—toward the true mean. The additional person is not changing the estimate very much. *Since everyone in Pittsburgh is about the same height, you don't need a big sample to get a good estimate of average height!*

But what if your data are really spread out? What if people in Pittsburgh are really anywhere from 3' to 7' tall? If you measure ten people at random, you might end up with an average height estimate that is 5'7"—or 6'3" or 4'5". If you added ten more people to your sample, the average you calculate would change a lot relative to what you are measuring. One really short person or one really tall person could shift the sample average quite a bit. It takes a lot more observations to settle on an estimate that does not shift much with the addition of one person. It is at that point that you are close to the true mean. The point of all this is that if your population data are very varied, with a wide distribution, you will need a larger sample in order to have a good sample. If your population data are very similar, with a tighter distribution, you will need a smaller sample size.

How do we incorporate this reasoning into sample size? With standard deviation of the population. Remember how the standard deviation measures the spread of our data? If the standard deviation is small relative to what we are measuring, the data are tightly clustered around the mean. If the standard deviation is large relative to what we are measuring, the data are *not* tightly clustered around the mean. If you need to remind yourself of what they would look like, refer back to Figures 6–1 and 6–2 (pages 78–79), the pictures of a wide distribution and a narrow distribution, respectively.

Now comes the statement that everyone makes at this point: well, if I knew the standard deviation of the population, then I would also know the true average of the population and I wouldn't need a sample in the first place!!! Arrrgghhh! That is true. You won't have the standard deviation of the population. So we have to use something that is a good guess. One way to get a good guess is to use the standard deviation of data from a similar data set. Let's say, for example, that I want to sample people in Austin, Texas, to determine the average income in the city. If I need the standard deviation to figure out what sample size is appropriate, I might look at data from the previous year in Austin or at data from another city, such as San Antonio. Of course, these data are not going to be a perfect match, but all I need is a good guess.

Another option is to pre-sample. This is where the analyst might start the research by taking a small sample first, determining its standard deviation, and using that standard deviation as the guess. Or you have to simply make your best guess, and use sensitivity analysis to determine what seems reasonable. Sensitivity analysis means that you would change your guess several times, plug the values into the formula to determine recommended sample sizes, and see how sensitive the result is to your changes.

The formula

Did I say "formula"? Yes! Yes, there is a simple formula that brings these three components together:

$$\left(\frac{t\text{-score associated with the chosen confidence level} \times \text{standard deviation guess}}{\text{Acceptable margin of error}}\right)^2.$$

To calculate the appropriate sample size for your study, you only need to plug in the values for these three components—confidence level, *t*-score, and standard deviation—and *square the result.* If you are familiar with math, you'll see that on the top, the higher the confidence level, the higher the *t*-value and the higher the resultant sample size. In the same vein, the higher the standard deviation guess, the higher the resultant sample size. On the bottom, the higher the acceptable margin of error, the lower the resultant sample size. Let's walk through an example of estimating a sample size:

Let's say we want to survey the citizens of Traer, Iowa, to ask about their satisfaction with public safety. We'll ask them to rate their satisfaction on a scale from 0 to 100, with 0 being entirely dissatisfied and 100 being completely satisfied in all respects. We can't survey everyone because Traer is too large, so we need to take a sample instead. But how big should the sample be? We can use the formula.

First, we would fall back on the standard confidence level used in most analysis, 95%, and from that we know to use the associated *t*-score of 1.96. Where could we go to get a standard deviation to use in our estimate for a good survey size? Let us assume that the nearby town of Toledo, Iowa, used the same survey last year. So let's steal from them. The standard deviation from Toledo last year was 17 points. Traer's city council is pretty picky, and it wants the margin of error to be only plus or minus 2 points. Here is a summary of the information that we need:

Confidence level: 95%
Associated *t*-score: 1.96
Guessed standard deviation: 17 points
Acceptable margin of error: 2 points

What do you get if you plug these values into the formula? Try it. I got a recommended sample size of 278.

$$\left(\frac{1.96 \times 17}{2} \right)^2$$

After all this explanation, it appears that appropriate sample size is really a matter of choice and the nature of the underlying data—with one major exception. Even if you're seeking high confidence and a low margin of error and the data seem to have a high standard deviation, once a sample size reaches around 1,000 or so, it will be large enough for most studies. Why? Because even though your choices seem to require a higher sample size, after about 1,000 observations, additional observations will not affect the estimate very much, so going for a larger and larger sample is not really worth the effort. In fact, when analysts use a 95% confidence level, the standard, acceptable sample size hovers around 350–450! This is why major national surveys need only a small number of people! If I want to determine presidential approval ratings, I don't have to ask a million people across the United States, even though our population is, at the time of this writing, 308,916,846. I need only several hundred people at worst and maybe a thousand or so at best! In fact, if I gather more and more data, I may end up with a sample that shows small patterns or differences that are statistically significant but not materially significant. Researchers working with huge data sets can actually be encumbered because they can see the detail in everything, which makes it difficult to identify the truly important relationships.

> At most, to get a good estimate, you need a sample of only about 1,000 for a population of 100 million. We just aren't that different.

I want to end this chapter with an example that pulls all these concepts together. In most newspapers that show polls about upcoming elections and the popularity of candidates, a note at the bottom or to the side of the poll gives the details about the methodology and all the assumptions underlying the survey. On July 29, 2009, a *New York Times* poll showed President Obama with a 58% approval rating. That is, when asked if they approved of what Obama was doing as president, 58% of respondents agreed. Here is the detail of the methodology of the poll, as printed in the paper:

How the Poll Was Conducted

The latest New York Times/CBS News poll is based on telephone interviews conducted July 24 through July 28 with 1,050 adults throughout the United States.

The sample of land-line telephone exchanges called was randomly selected by a computer from a complete list of more than 69,000 active residential exchanges across the country. The exchanges were chosen so as to ensure that each region of the country was represented in proportion to its population.

Within each exchange, random digits were added to form a complete telephone number, thus permitting access to listed and unlisted numbers alike. Within each household, one adult was designated by a random procedure to be the respondent for the survey.

To increase coverage, this land-line sample was supplemented by respondents reached through random dialing of cellphone numbers. The two samples were then combined.

The combined results have been weighted to adjust for variation in the sample relating to geographic region, sex, race, Hispanic origin, marital status, age and education. In addition, the land-line respondents were weighted to take account of household size and number of telephone lines into the residence, while the cellphone respondents were weighted according to whether they were reachable only by cellphone or also by land line.

In theory, in 19 cases out of 20, overall results based on such samples will differ by no more than three percentage points in either direction from what would have been obtained by seeking to interview all American adults. For smaller subgroups, the margin of sampling error is larger. Shifts in results between polls over time also have a larger sampling error.

In addition to sampling error, the practical difficulties of conducting any survey of public opinion may introduce other sources of error into the poll. Variation in the wording and order of questions, for example, may lead to somewhat different results.[1]

---

1   Reprinted with permission from "How the Poll Was Conducted," *New York Times,* July 29, 2009, http://www.nytimes.com/2009/07/30/us/politics/30mbox.html?_r = 1 (accessed March 3, 2010).

The margin of error that the surveyors chose to use was plus or minus 3 percentage points. The newspaper doesn't explicitly say so, but the confidence level chosen was 95%. In theory this means that in 1 out of 20 cases, the estimated approval rating from the survey would fall outside of the margin of error; in other words, the conclusion from the survey would be wrong. We can be 95% confident that Obama's true approval rating, on the day of the survey, was somewhere between 55% and 61% (3 percentage points above and below our sample mean of 58%).

> ## Random sampling is the gold standard in surveying.
> ## Always go with random sampling unless you absolutely,
> ## positively need to do otherwise.

There are a few other things that are interesting about this poll. Obviously, the pollsters were concerned about who was represented in the sample. If a sample is chosen completely at random, every person in the population has an equal chance of being included. And it is likely that the resulting sample will include about the same proportion of men, women, African Americans, whites, Asians, etc., that are in the entire population. But if you want to make sure that there is an equal proportion, you can break your sample into those groups and randomly sample within them (called "stratified sampling," as in taking a sample of dirt from different strata in a rock face). Another option is to weigh the responses of people in a particular group so that their collective response has the same relative impact as their group in the population. That is, you can make the response of an African American carry more importance in estimating the survey results, if you want. This type of manipulation of the sample is best left to professional surveyors, but educated consumers of survey information should know for whom the survey is speaking. Remember that anytime you try to construct a sample rather than have it chosen at random from the population, you introduce bias.

The article also mentions that the survey was done via telephone, and it highlights one of the biggest problems with survey methodology today: cell phones. Traditional telephone surveys are done by randomly calling people with phones. It was easy enough to get phone numbers from the phone directories. We have known for a long time that this excludes those without phones and those with unlisted numbers—a relatively small proportion of the overall population. But there is no directory of cell phone numbers. If I tried to follow the traditional telephone methodology, paying a company to provide me with a random list of numbers in a particular area code, the number of people without landline phones would grow, and young adults would be excluded almost entirely. In my most recent graduate statistics course, out of 30 students, only 2 had landline phones.

You might think that simply choosing numbers at random would be easy, and it would capture both landlines and cell phones. But think about the costs involved in surveying. Every phone call to a nonexistent, commercial, or disconnected line takes time, and time is money. Establishing a random list of numbers to call would include a sizable proportion of bad numbers. The problem is extreme if you have a specific group that you want to survey, such as teens who use the local swimming pool. How are you going to locate all the cell phone numbers from which you could draw a random sample? Just dialing numbers at random and hoping you catch a teen who has been to the local pool would be a tremendous waste of time. The *New York Times* poll explains how it tries to get around this problem: by using landlines for most of the survey and cell phones for part of it. It is as good an effort as one can make, but as cell phone use continues to grow in our country, the problem will only get worse.

The art (not science) of gathering information that is valid and reliable needs to evolve with technology and social trends. Recently, I advised a nonprofit on how to reach former college scholarship recipients. We were unsuccessful in locating contact information for a number of the former students. However, an inspired survey director decided to locate them via Facebook. I established a Facebook page for the purposes of contacting the students and was able to reach three more within 24 hours.

I'll end on an important point. All samples have a margin of error, and we tend to ignore it. But you shouldn't forget that the margin of error is there. Analysts never really can give an exact estimate; they should always report a range—the average plus or minus the margin of error—and make sure that the audience knows the range. This comes up when, in political races, polls show two candidates with support percentages that are close together. If a poll shows that Candidate A has support of 48% of the electorate and Candidate B has support of 50% of the electorate, and if you like Candidate B, you might think yay, we're winning! But don't be too confident. With a 3% margin of error, the true value for candidate A could be between 45% and 51%, and the true value for candidate B could be between 47% and 53%. Those two ranges overlap. If the true value for Candidate A were 51% and the true value for Candidate B were 49%, all those celebratory Candidate B supporters would be very disappointed when the actual results came in. Don't confuse all polls, or all samples, with reality. They are only *estimates!*

"Here are the last of the paper surveys. Couldn't we have just done this some easier way?" Sharon was crabby. She had been recruited into helping input survey data, and was not happy about having to step away from her end-of-year accounting preparation. Council Top had decided that as long as it was going to survey its volunteer firefighters, it might as well contact other jurisdictions to see if they wanted to participate.

In the end, the city had sampled 400 volunteer firefighters from around the entire southwest corner of the state. About half, 205, had responded quickly to the e-mail request to go to the survey Web page. Those surveys were recorded automatically and immediately.

Nina was thrilled with how easy it was. The formatting was easy. So was creating the questions and controlling the answer selection. For example, she really wanted to know what people thought about their volunteer firefighter experience, so she did not want to let respondents have the option of answering "neutral," or 3 on a 7-point scale. So she allowed the survey to include only "very positive," "positive," "somewhat positive," "somewhat negative," "negative," and "very negative." And . . . it was free! You only had to pay if you wanted some special analyses done.

The jurisdictions involved had a lot of members without e-mail addresses—or if the firefighter had one, the jurisdiction did not have it on record in any central location. But all of them had addresses that could be easily tracked through the water billing system. So in addition to sending out a notice to those with e-mail addresses, Nina sent out postcards with the Web address for the survey, and then finally sent out a follow-up mailing, including the survey and a self-addressed stamped envelope and a free "Firefighters Are Hot" bumper sticker, to those who had still not responded. She knew that any type of incentive would increase response rates: people felt too guilty about getting something for nothing to ignore the request to return the survey. The paper surveys came in much slower, and Sharon had been working at inputting the responses from them.

"We ended up with 87 paper surveys. None has come in for six days. Do you want me to keeping checking the mailroom?" Sharon clearly did not want to have to check with the mailroom again.

"No, we have to cut off the responses at some point so we can start the analysis. And adding the 87 to our original 205, we have 292 total. That is 292/400… a response rate of 73%. That's fantastic!" Nina could hardly contain her excitement.

Sharon looked at her for a moment, half laughed, half snickered, and said, "Well, I'm glad someone is excited about this. Didn't you have to throw out a bunch?"

"Yeah, you're right. The overall response rate was 73%, but we had to throw out the ones from retired firefighters. Whether they were satisfied with their work situation 15 years ago doesn't help us much now."

"How did they get mixed in?" Sharon sat down.

"Some towns added new volunteers to their rolls but never cleaned off the names of people who no longer were volunteers. You would think that it would be easy to pull together a list of current volunteer firefighters and their contact information, but fewer than half the towns could do it. The others all had problems. It took me three weeks to clean up the list, and even then, a lot of bad names or contact information got through. If you throw out the retirees and look at only usable surveys, the response rate goes down to 54%. But that is still really good."

"Can you mix the results from the paper and the electronic surveys? Is that against the rules or something?"

"Actually, if we were doing scientific research of the highest standard, we probably wouldn't want to mix the results since people who respond electronically are different in a systematic way from those who respond to paper surveys. But for our purposes, it shouldn't be a big problem. We can compare the responses from the two groups and see if there is a difference, and if there is, we can see whether it is big enough to really matter. If there is a difference, I bet it is due to age. We ask people's age, so we'll be able to test that hypothesis."

Sharon stood up. "Do you need me anymore?" Her interest in survey methodology was clearly waning.

"Uh, no. Thank you very much, Sharon."

"Sure. Anytime." Sharon disappeared down the hallway. Nina suspected that Sharon would stop at the smoking spot outside the back of the building on her way back to her desk. She turned back to the computer. Setting up and running the survey had taken four weeks. She only had a week in which to produce the draft report. She had already prepared the intro, background, and methodology sections while waiting for the survey results. She just needed to plug in the results, conclusions, and recommendations and write an executive summary. Plenty of time.

Review questions

1. What are the three frames by which to determine an adequate sample size?

2. What is a margin of error? How does a small margin of error affect the sample size?

3. If you want to obtain a very precise estimate, how would that affect your margin of error and sample size?

4. Create your own example to determine an appropriate sample size. Use the formula on page 94.

5. What are the benefits of a large sample size? What are the possible drawbacks?

6. Describe three possible alternatives to using landline telephones to conduct surveys, and explain how each might affect your response rate.

    a.

    b.

    c.

7. What is stratified sampling, and when might you use this technique?

8. Which of the three options below is the most appropriate way to determine an adequate sample size? Explain why the others are inappropriate.

    a. Take 10% of the population and use that number.

    b. Use the three frames to determine the sample size.

    c. Look at other research on the topic and use the same sample size.

9. Describe the relationship between precision and margin of error. Why is it important when sampling a population?

10. Look at the article about the survey taken to determine President Obama's approval rating. What can you assume about the margin of error, precision, and overall reliability and validity of this survey?

Can We PLEASE Start to Actually Conclude Something?

[DRAWING CONCLUSIONS WITH NOMINAL OR ORDINAL DATA]

"I'm not sure what to do with this survey data." The summer intern appeared at Nina's cubicle entrance (it couldn't really be called a door).

Nina took a deep breath before turning around. The intern was really, really trying to be helpful, but Nina was wondering if having an intern was actually a help or if she should add a new line, "hand holder," under her own job description. No, if she complained to Chuck, he would probably laugh and say it would just fit under "and other duties as assigned." She should have asked that that line be taken off the description before she accepted the job offer.

What was she thinking?! She loved this job. And the intern really wasn't that bad; in fact, she asked great questions and had already suggested new ways to present data to the council. It was just that she worked so quickly that as soon as Nina gave her one job, she seemed to be done within minutes, asking for the next task.

"We need to put the data into some tables to see if there are differences between professional and volunteer firefighters. Let me see if I can show you an example." Nina started searching her computer file folders for some old electronic files.

"Do you mean some contingency tables and cross tabs?" asked Maria.

"Yes!" Nina spun around. "Are you familiar with how to set those up?" Wow! The intern knew about contingency tables! Things were looking up.

"Sure, we worked with lots of qualitative data in my research assistantship. Do you want chi squares run, too?"

"Yes!" Nina squeaked. She couldn't keep the excitement out of her voice. "It would be such a big help if you could run contingency tables for each survey question. I know it will take a long time to do each one, but I also know that some councilperson sometime, somewhere, will want to know how the responses to each question break down between volunteers and professional firefighters. I would rather be prepared with all the results than not have the answer at the meeting. Otherwise we end up delaying decisions for yet another week while we run more and more numbers."

Maria was almost a little smug in her response. "Actually, you can run all the contingency tables and cross tabs at once with an option in the stats software we use in our grad program. It will only take a couple of minutes. I'll run them, and then after lunch we can sit down and go over the ones that are statistically significant."

"Now I'm really feeling old." Nina was starting to hate Maria. "Maybe I should think about getting that software. It takes *for-ev-er* in my spreadsheet program."

"It's a student license. The full license is pretty expensive, I think. It would probably be cheaper to just keep hiring student interns," laughed Maria as she stepped away to her own cubicle.

"But could I keep up with them?" thought Nina.

S ometimes it is hard to keep up with how all this information fits together. Let me review where we started in this book, where we are, and what is coming in the last few chapters.

Where have we been?

We started out with research design in general and talked about the importance of a good design. I outlined the two key concepts in research design: (1) validity—are we measuring what we want to measure (i.e., the idea of accuracy)? and (2) reliability— is our design good enough to be replicated so that different researchers doing the same study would get the same results (i.e., the idea of precision)? The concept of validity is especially important. We want to make sure that we are testing the right relationship or answering the right question for our needs.

> Step 1: Ask a good question.
> Step 2: Get good data to answer the question.
> Step 3: Use good methods to answer the question.
> Step 4: Return to Step 1.

We also went over how to move from a general research topic to a general research question, and then to a specific research question. We talked about building a hypothesis that we can test with data.

Ah, data! Before we even got to a fact or a number, there was so much to talk about concerning data! We discussed the difficulty of operationalizing a concept into nominal, ordinal, and/or interval data that can be measured and summarized in some way. We also talked about how the concept of validity can be applied to a measure as much as it is applied to the research design. When we measure a concept with data, we need to ask if our chosen measure is really measuring what we want it to measure. For example, if you want to measure how "rich" someone is, should you use income, assets, net worth? What is considered "income"?

And then we jumped right in and discussed collecting data and describing them through descriptive statistics. What is a typical value in our data (measures of central tendency: mean, median, and mode)? How spread out are our data (measures of dispersion)? Is there anything weird about the data (outliers, skew), and if so, can we still use the data in further analysis? (The answer is yes, through the beauty of the normal curve and the central limit theorem.) How can I understand where a single point is relative to the rest of the data (z-scores and associated percentages)?

If we have a complete population of data, we can stop right there. It is what it is. There are no guesses, no likelihoods, no doubts, no concept of statistical significance. But how often do we have every piece of information for our research question? Not often. We usually use samples, and with sampling comes uncertainty: we have only estimates and sample error. To understand this uncertainty, we had to discuss probability and confidence and statistical significance.

These three concepts—probability, confidence, and statistical significance—must be understood if you want to move to one of the most basic questions in any kind of analysis: is there a difference between this and that? Is there likely to be a difference between a sample and the population? Is there a big difference between a single point and the rest of the data? Is there a difference between two groups? These questions are at the heart of inferential statistics, where we use *t*-scores instead of *z*-scores, have confidence intervals around our estimates, and decide on the confidence level we need to reach before we feel safe enough to draw conclusions. Inferential statistics allows us to infer something about a population from the data we have in hand in a sample. (To infer is just another way of saying to guess, to estimate, or to conclude.)

Research is basically asking if there is a difference between this and that.

The first of these concepts is probability, and we learned how a probability is just a ratio, a percentage, a fraction, and how there are a number of ways in which you can obtain a particular outcome over all the possible outcomes. Probability is key to inferential statistics because, since probability is a guess or an estimate, there is always a chance that our guess or estimate is wrong. We need to understand basic probability in order to understand the likelihood that we are right or, conversely, that we are wrong.

The second concept, confidence, is the natural next step. There are two ways analysts use confidence: with confidence intervals and with confidence levels.

Confidence intervals are the same as margins of error. With samples, we are making estimates, right? And we know that the estimates are not perfect; we hope that the real value is somewhere close to our estimate. So we explicitly place boundaries around our estimate to mark the level of error that we are comfortable accepting. Are we comfortable estimating average income and giving ourselves a margin of error of plus or minus $5,000? Or is that too broad? Would we be more comfortable with an estimate that has a margin of error of plus or minus only $1,000? What we decide will help us determine our sample size.

Confidence is also used in establishing a confidence level. Once we know how likely it is that we are right (or wrong), we can express our level of confidence in our result. Confidence is not just the measure of the likelihood of being right or wrong in our estimate; it is also the standard we *choose,* as analysts, to apply to the probabilities. This is where judgment and subjectivity come in, and suddenly we realize that the field of statistics can be as open to personal interpretation as art or music. How much evidence is enough to draw a conclusion and make a decision? How sure do you need to be in your estimate? The same numerical probability of being right or wrong can be acceptable to one analyst, who draws a conclusion that x is different from $y,$ and not acceptable to another, who draws the conclusion that there is not enough evidence to say that x is different from $y.$ It all depends on the standard being applied. Sometimes, when you have a difficult but important policy question, such as the impact of a home situation on long-term educational outcomes, you might be willing to accept a lower standard of evidence simply because the cause-and-effect relationship is very difficult to disentangle from other relationships. One researcher may accept a lower level of confidence simply to be able to advance programs. Another researcher may want to apply a higher standard, requiring that a higher level of confidence be reached before any policy decisions or changes can be made. (Remember: we are always talking about a relatively high level of confidence in all cases. The choice is usually between using a standard level of 90%, 95%, or 99% confidence.)

Where are we now, and where are we going?

We are now at the point where we go beyond asking if there is a difference. We are asking if one thing is related to another. In other words, is there some tie between how one thing behaves and how another behaves? We have danced around this question already in this book. We have asked whether there is a link between weather and weapons in Iraq and whether there is a link between professional status and fire deaths. We are entering the world of testing for associations and, eventually, causal relationships.

We will first do this with just two variables—two series of data about something, like the number of rainy days (first thing) and the number of guns found at military checkpoints (second thing). But nothing in life is that easy. Relationships, whether between people or data, are much more complicated. By the end of this book, we will be looking at relationships between two series of data while controlling for other things going on at the same time. We will be able to separate out the impact of something like rainy days from everything else that might be affecting the number of guns at a checkpoint.

How are we going to do this? PATTERNS! Statistics, and for that matter, most research, is simply based on patterns in data. And usually we are looking for patterns that are similar to, or in direct contrast with, one another. For those of you who have kept track of material from the first chapter, we worked from a general topic idea down to very specific research questions. We talked about using measures—data—to operationalize the concepts we dealt with. We might have even formed hypotheses, or guesses, about what we thought the relationships would be. We are now at the point where we can test those hypotheses! Aren't you excited?! Ok, maybe I expect too much from people who are less geeky than I am. But what this does mean is that we are at the point where we can come up with some results, and for most people, that is an exciting time.

Associations and co-movement

It is important to distinguish here between association and causal relationships, and to review some material that we introduced in Chapter 1. In Chapter 1, we talked about models of how different variables relate to each other. We are going to return to those models because we are now at the point where we can actually test our hypotheses!

An association is weaker than a relationship (just as an acquaintanceship is less strong than a friendship). Basically, an association means that there is co-movement between the variables: when one moves, so does the other. There are two kinds of co-movement: positive and negative.

With a positive association, the two variables move in the same direction. That is, when one variable goes up, the other goes up. When one goes down, the other goes down. When the values in one increase, the values in the other increase, too. The values don't have to increase by the same amount or at the same rate; it is the pattern of movement that matters. The two streams of data move in concert: ↓↓ ↑↑

With a negative association, the two variables move in opposite directions. That is, when one variable goes up, the other variable goes down: ↓↑ ↑↓

If, when one variable changes, there is no change in the second, we know that there is no association between the two.

Moving from co-movement to causality

Maybe there is an association, but is there causality? That is, just because things move in the same direction does not mean that they are really and truly linked. Using the example in Chapter 1 of Popsicles and the level of murders, we realized that while the amount of Popsicle consumption and the number of murders might co-vary—that is, there might be an association where both move in a positive or negative direction together—there is not a causal relationship between the two. Remember, to support the claim that one thing affects another—for example, that job training programs for prison inmates reduce recidivism—you must have four things:

1. Time order

2. Theoretical support

3. Co-variation

4. No spuriousness.

At this point, where we want to actually test to see if a relationship exists, the theory is particularly important because it helps us identify what we consider to be the dependent variable and the independent variable(s). The dependent variable is the variable that depends on the other variable(s)—go figure! If you were an English major long ago in your college days, it is like the direct object of a sentence: it is the thing being affected. The independent variables are what influence or act on the dependent variable. Let's go back to one of the illustrations we had at the beginning of the book.

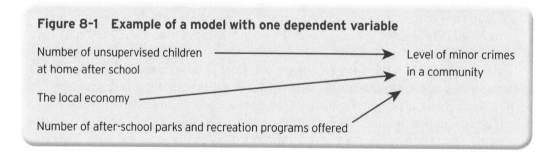

Figure 8-1   Example of a model with one dependent variable

Number of unsupervised children at home after school

The local economy

Number of after-school parks and recreation programs offered

Level of minor crimes in a community

In this example, the dependent variable is the level of minor crimes in a community. We want to understand what is influencing those crimes. Why are they going up (or down)? The three factors we have listed—number of unsupervised children at home after school, the local economy, and number of after-school parks and recreation programs offered—are all things that we think influence the minor crime rate. They are all independent variables in this model. They all have arrows going out of them; they are influencing other things. The level of minor crimes is the recipient of the arrows; it is being affected *by* these other things. There is only one dependent variable in each model. Here, you can look at the relationships one by one, or you can look at all of them at the same time. However, if you draw a model and it looks like Figure 8–2, you are in for more work.

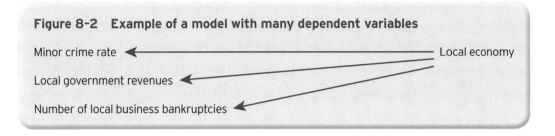

Figure 8-2   Example of a model with many dependent variables

In this example, there are three dependent variables and only one independent variable. Again, you can look at them one by one, but in this case, you can't look at this as a single model. For a single model, we need to have only one dependent variable. Looking at data for the sketch above means looking at three separate models.

Let's go back to the first, better model (Figure 8–1). We can now add in our hypotheses about whether the relationship between each independent variable and the dependent variable is positive or negative.

Table 8-1   Variables and hypothesized relationships in model

Independent variable	Dependent variable	Hypothesized nature of relationship
Number of unsupervised children at home after school	Level of minor crime in the community	Positive: As the number of unsupervised children goes up, the level of minor crime goes up.
The local economy	Level of minor crime in the community	Negative: As the local economy grows, the level of minor crime in the community decreases.
Number of after-school parks and recreation programs offered	Level of minor crime in the community	Negative: As the number of after-school parks and recreation programs offered increases, the level of minor crime in the community decreases.

Geez, enough review! Can we get to testing for causal relationships already?

Yes, we can. Let's get to it. We can focus on six main questions when testing for relationships, with the normal English-language version up front and the statistical analyst–language version in parentheses:

1. Is there a similar pattern in the two sets of data? (Is there an association between the variables?)

2. If so, how strong is it? (What is the strength of the association?)

3. Is there a relationship between the two variables? (Is one variable having an impact on another? Do you think there may be causality?)

4. If so, what kind of relationship? (What is the direction and nature of that relationship? Which is the dependent and which is the independent variable?)

5. If so, is it statistically significant? (Is that relationship statistically significant?)

6. If so, does it really matter? (Is that relationship materially significant?)

These six questions are the basis for the rest of this book. We will walk through common ways to answer them. Let's start with the first one: is there a similar pattern in the two sets of data? The first step in knowing how to answer the question is to understand your data. What kind of data do you have? The methods you use to look for associations and relationships, and the tests you use to understand if those relationships are significant, depend on the nature of the data.

Table 8-2   Types of data and tests used in everyday statistics

Kind of data	Method used to look for relationships	Is there a pattern? What is its strength?	Is it significant?	Does it really matter?
Interval	Regression	r and r^2	t-tests, F-tests	Up to your audience
Ordinal	Contingency tables/cross tabs	Gamma, Tau, Somers' D	Chi square (X^2)	
Nominal	Contingency tables/cross tabs	Lambda, Cramer's V	Chi square (X^2)	

I know I hear a sigh of relief from the reader at this point, because you notice that you have already covered one item in the table above: t-tests. T-tests allow us to determine if there is a statistically significant difference, measured by a t-score (surprise!) between two things: an observation and the rest of a population, a sample and a population, or two samples. Or is it a gasp I hear, because you think you have to learn about things like Gammas and Lambdas, F-tests, and other letters of the Greek alphabet? Rest assured, dear reader. Yes, we will learn about how some of these things work—for example, we will briefly talk about F-scores at the end of Chapter 9—but most common statistical software programs do the math for you. Your job is to be able to interpret the results, and luckily, the results are interpreted through the same lenses of confidence that we have already covered.

When you have nominal or ordinal data

For the rest of this chapter, we will walk through how to understand if two things represented by nominal or ordinal data are associated. We will save interval data for the next chapter.

If you remember, nominal data (sometimes called categorical data) are data that are represented as members of a group or category. There is no set interval or relative value between the different members. For example, the different flavors of ice cream are categorical data. There is no set value between chocolate, vanilla, butter pecan, or mint chocolate chip. We can only count the members of these groups. Of course, you will be able to count the number of people who prefer vanilla over chocolate, but the actual group of vanilla has no numerical value in and of itself.

Remember that ordinal data are data for which there is not a set value to different groups or a set interval between groups, but you can rank order the groups. For example, when you do a survey and ask citizens about their level of satisfaction with local government services, you might ask if they are highly satisfied, satisfied, unsatisfied, or very unsatisfied. These categories have a value in relation to each other, but we can't really measure the difference between satisfied and unsatisfied. If you have these types of data, you analyze relationships with contingency tables. Now the steps:

Step 1: Determine which is the independent variable and which is the dependent variable

A contingency table has one variable listed across the top and another listed down the left side. The first step in setting up a table is go back to your original model and ask yourself which is the dependent variable and which is the independent variable. The independent variable is across the top, comprising the columns. The dependent variable is down the side, comprising the rows.

Step 2: Set up the contingency table

Start with putting in the frequencies in each cell as appropriate. This produces a contingency table, as shown in Table 8–3.

Table 8-3   Contingency table of solid-waste pickup service and citizen satisfaction

Average citizen rating for service quality	Type of solid-waste pickup service		
	Backyard pickup	Curbside pickup	Total
Satisfied or very satisfied	300	25	325
Unsatisfied or very unsatisfied	50	125	175
Total	350	150	500

This table shows the results of a survey of 500 residents in Council Top, Iowa. Council Top has two types of solid-waste pickup service. In the older part of town, backyard pickup has existed for over 40 years; yes, believe it or not, in some towns, the solid-waste workers will walk around to the back of the house, carry the bins to the truck, and then return the bins to the back of the house. Newer areas of town, as they have been built, have had to settle for curbside pickup. The manager, Chuck Edwards, wanted to see if there might be any way to show his council that citizens with curbside pickup were just as satisfied with solid-waste services as those with backyard pickup; if so, the entire town could be converted to curbside pickup (he hoped with trucks that would have mechanical arms, or the "one-armed bandits," which also tend to need only one employee on them instead of two—the savings were so tempting!). While he didn't say so directly, he was really asking if service type (the independent variable) had an impact on satisfaction (the dependent variable).

You may already be able to see that Chuck is going to be disappointed, but let's give him all the numbers and see if there really is a relationship between solid-waste service type and citizen satisfaction.

Step 3: Convert the frequencies to cross tabs (short for cross tabulations) and compare across tables

It can be hard to make good comparisons with raw numbers. In this case, the sizes of the two groups are different. There are many more customers served by backyard pickup than by curbside pickup. To **standardize** the numbers so that we can compare them easily, we convert the cells into percentiles *going down*. In each column, the cells in the table now show the percentiles for each row category. The percentiles can be added as you go down the column to reach 100%. Table 8–4 shows how we would convert Chuck's table.

Table 8-4   Cross tab of solid-waste pickup service and citizen satisfaction

Average citizen rating for service quality	Type of solid-waste pickup service		
	Backyard pickup (%)	Curbside pickup (%)	Total (%)
Satisfied or very satisfied	86	17	65
Unsatisfied or very unsatisfied	14	83	35
Total	100	100	100

Now comparisons are much easier. From this table, we can tell Chuck the bad news. We can break the news to him in a variety of ways:

- More than 85% of citizens with backyard pickup are satisfied with their service, compared to only 17% of curbside pickup citizens.

- There is a 69-point difference in the percentage of citizens who are satisfied with backyard pickup compared to those who are satisfied with curbside pickup.

- Backyard pickup customers are over four times more likely to be satisfied with their solid-waste service than curbside pickup customers.

Percentage down, compare across.

But perhaps Chuck is not going to bring up the differences after all; if he did, he could end up with all citizens getting backyard pickup! He might want to emphasize just that the majority of citizens, 65%, are happy with their solid-waste service. Without knowing it, Chuck has gone through four of our questions on associations and causality:

1. Is there a similar pattern in the two sets of data? (Is there an association between the variables?)

   Based on the cross tabs, it sure seems like there is a pattern in the data. The variable along the top, type of solid-waste service, is nominal. The satisfaction rating data is ordinal. The cells with the lower percentages go across the table on one diagonal, while the cells with the larger numbers go in the other direction on another diagonal.

2. If so, how strong is it? (What is the strength of the association?)

   The strongest relationship is a perfect relationship. No, not marriage advice, and I doubt that there are any perfect relationships out there, anyway. In statistics, a perfect relationship is one in which one variable is perfectly correlated with another. Huh? That means that if you know one variable, you can predict the other variable with 100% success. They move together perfectly and predictably: if you know the

Table 8-5 Example of cross tab of solid-waste pickup service and citizen satisfaction with a perfect relationship

Average citizen rating for service quality	Type of solid-waste pickup service		
	Backyard pickup	Curbside pickup	Total
Satisfied or very satisfied	350 (100%)	0 (0%)	350 (65%)
Unsatisfied or very unsatisfied	0 (0%)	150 (100%)	150 (35%)
Total	350 (100%)	150 (100%)	500 (100%)

value of one, you know the value of the other. Well, a perfect relationship to give Chuck nightmares would be one shown in Table 8–5 (frequencies in parentheses).

The weakest relationship, on the other hand, is the one where there is no difference across the percentages in the different columns of the independent variable, as shown in Table 8–6.

Table 8-6   Example of cross tab of solid-waste pickup service and citizen satisfaction with no relationship

Average citizen rating for service quality	Type of solid-waste pickup service		
	Backyard pickup	Curbside pickup	Total
Satisfied or very satisfied	228 (65%)	98 (65%)	326 (65%)
Unsatisfied or very unsatisfied	122 (35%)	52 (35%)	174 (35%)
Total	350 (100%)	150 (100%)	500 (100%)

Here, it doesn't matter if you have backyard or curbside pickup. In both cases, about two-thirds of the citizens are satisfied and about one-third are not. The statistics called Lambda and Cramer's V and others actually try to numerically measure the strength of the association with ordinal and nominal data. Those measures are beyond the scope of this book, but they are in the software programs if you want them. For most purposes in state and local government work, simply comparing the percentages will be enough for your audience.

3. Do you think that there is a relationship between the two variables? (Is one variable having an impact on another? Do you think there may be causality?)

   Chuck has a theory that the type of solid-waste service the citizen has and that citizen's satisfaction with the service are not just associated, but related.

4. If so, what kind of relationship? (What is the direction and nature of that relationship? Which is the dependent and which is the independent variable?)

   This is a no-brainer. Chuck thinks that the type of service has an influence, an impact, on service satisfaction. Service type is the independent variable; satisfaction is the dependent variable.

5. If so, is it statistically significant? (Is that relationship statistically significant?)

   Ah, now we are in new territory. In this book, we already talked about how one could determine if two groups were statistically significantly different through *t*-scores. How can one do it with nominal or ordinal data? Through a measure called the chi square, or X^2. Chi square compares the actual frequencies in your table with the frequencies you would expect if there were no relationship. For Chuck, it would be comparing the actual data he has in his table with what he would have in the No Relationship example in Table 8–6. Again, the calculations are beyond the scope of this text, but the result is a chi square value. This value is not important in and of itself, but it is associated with a p value. YAY! Now we are back to something familiar! Remember how "for every t, there is a p?" Well, in the same way, for every chi square value, there is an associated p value.

The p values are interpreted in the same way as before. The p value indicates the likelihood that the data would fall out the way they do in the table *if there were no relationship* between the two variables. How likely is it that the data would appear in the table as they do just randomly? Luckily, the computer software programs calculate the p values for us when they calculate the chi squares. The higher the chi square value, the lower the p value (if you remember, just like the higher the t, the lower the p). If you are using a 95% confidence level as your standard and you have a p value at or below .05, you could say that you are at least 95% confident that there is a relationship between the two variables.

In Chuck's case, the chi square value for his original table is 220, with an associated p value of .000. We can say that there is virtually no chance that Chuck got these survey results at random, virtually no chance that there is no relationship. In fact, we can say with almost 100% confidence that there *is* a relationship and that the type of solid-waste service does have an influence on citizen satisfaction ratings.

6. If so, does it really matter? (Is that relationship materially significant?)

Well, to Chuck, it does. This is a judgment call. But I don't need to have numbers backing me up to say that the difference seems large enough, in percentage point terms, to show that backyard pickup is a lot more popular than curbside pickup—and that Chuck is going to be stuck with backyard solid-waste pickup for a long time.

"What did you find?" Nina was tired and cranky by the end of the day, but she was trying to shrug it off. She had been working with the budget office all day on a performance measurement report on home inspections, but some of the data were inconsistent with other departmental reports. She didn't understand why the numbers were different, and she had been trying to untangle the mess for hours. She was ready to throw up her hands, close her eyes, pick a report at random, and go with it for the official benchmark numbers.

"Here is the contingency table," said Maria, handing her one piece of paper (which you can see on page 116).

Table 8-7   Firefighter deaths contingency table

Type of duty	Career, no.	Volunteer, no.
Operating at fire ground	22	12
Responding to or returning from alarm	4	26
Other on duty	9	4
Training	7	5
Operating at nonfire emergencies	0	6
Totals	42	53

"And here is the cross tab."

Table 8-8   Firefighter deaths cross tab

Type of duty	Career, %	Volunteer, %
Operating at fire ground	52	23
Responding to or returning from alarm	10	49
Other on duty	21	8
Training	17	9
Operating at nonfire emergencies	0	11
Totals	100	100

"Is the difference statistically significant? Not that I am going to report that to the council," laughed Nina. "They would look at me as if I had horns on my head. But I would just be interested myself."

"I checked it, and no surprise, it is very statistically significant: p = .0000261. About no chance that you would get these numbers randomly."

"Well, I am not surprised, either. At least something today seems to have gone right the first time." Nina paused. "Do you know anything about home inspections, Maria?"

"No, but if it is about data, I'm willing to learn," Maria said.

"Here, let me show you what I am trying to figure out," said Nina. Under her breath, she muttered, "I *have* to get more interns."

Review questions

1. Explain the difference between co-movement and causality.

2. When looking for relationships, what is the method to be used with

    a. Nominal data?

    b. Ordinal data?

    c. Interval data?

3. What kind of data can be used in contingency tables?

4. Why are models important to review when you set up a contingency table?

5. Create an example of a contingency table, with the appropriate kind of variables for rows and columns. Explain why contingency tables are organized in this way.

6. What do we mean by "percentage down and compare across" in interpreting contingency tables?

7. Make up data to fill in the contingency table you made in Question #5, and explain the results in a paragraph.

8. Make up two examples of contingency tables, one showing a strong relationship and one showing a weak relationship.

9. How would you use a chi square value?

10. In Table 8-2 it states that whether a result really matters is up to the audience. What does this mean?

[DRAWING CONCLUSIONS WITH INTERVAL DATA]

"Well, that does it!" Nina was happy, although she shouldn't have been. The home inspection data were terrible, but she and Maria had finally figured out that one of the supervising inspectors had instructed his team to fill out the service reports using the wrong dates. The department was trying to keep track of the time taken to complete home inspections. It had been asked to record the dates of the initial request, first visit, and subsequent visits (if needed), and the date on which the building finally passed inspection. One of the teams seemed to be doing a great job with timeliness; its average completion time for the inspection process was lower than that of any of the other teams by almost four days—"a statistically significant difference," Nina remembered Maria saying. She and Maria wanted to know how this particular team did so well: why was it so different from the rest?

"It's easy to be better when you cook the books!" said Maria when they discovered the problem. It wasn't that the team had actually tried to report inaccurate data; the team had simply misunderstood the definition of "the date of initial request." They were supposed to record the date when the request for an inspection was first made to the department; instead, the wonder team interpreted it as the date when the request was forwarded to the team with an appointment. This allowed them to avoid counting the few days it took for the request to work its way through the department office staff.

"Thanks for all your help on this project, Maria," said Nina. "I really appreciate the time you took to go back and pull all those orders to get the right request dates. That team's scores are now in line with the rest; in fact, they are a little slower than most."

"Why do these inspections take so long to complete?" Maria asked, scrolling through the corrected data. "There are a couple in here that go for over three months.

Here is one that took over nine months to be completed!"

"Probably a lot of things—the size of the building, how old it is, the experience of the inspector, the number of fixes that need to be done. Lots of stuff, I guess."

"Hmmm. Some of these long ones are in the same couple of neighborhood developments. Do you think there is something going on there?"

"Maybe, but I don't know how you would sort it all out," replied Nina.

"All this information is in the database, correct? Building characteristics, who inspected them, location, number of initial problems, type of problems?" Maria was still moving the mouse all around the screen.

"Yeah.... What are you getting at?"

"Oh, I just wonder if we ran a regression on the data if the builder would pop out as statistically significant."

Regression?! Nina remembered some word like that back in her graduate school statistics class, but her brain had shut down by that point in the semester. She had glided through to the final in her course without having to spend too much brain power on those chapters.

"What is that again?" Nina tried to sound casual, as if she knew all about regression but just needed a moment to remember.

"We can look at all the various potential influences on the timeliness of inspections together. It isolates each of the relationships so that you can see what is statistically significant and what is not, and what kind of impact each variable has," said Maria.

"Oh, yeah, I remember now." Of course, Nina didn't. "If you want to play around with the data, I bet Chuck would be interested. He is really bugged by the never-ending complaints about inspections. If he had some data to show why things take so long, he might be able to get the council off that topic."

"Yeah, and onto rewriting the junk car ordinance!" laughed Maria.

"Or pushing the leash law." Nina's voice went low. "All cats must be on a four-foot leash at all times! And the animal control officers will be issued rulers," she joked in a poor attempt to imitate Chuck's voice. They both started sniggering. It was late, and they were getting goofy.

"No, no, I know…chickens! That is what he needs to tackle next. Council Top needs a new backyard chicken ordinance. We can have a public hearing and make it open to anyone, especially those who want to bring their own chickens to show how harmless they are."

"No, no, this is better … a leash law for in-town chickens!!" Nina and Maria almost collapsed with laughter. "And licenses–all chickens must be licensed, with photos! And chipped! They have to be chipped! So that if the chicken crosses the road and doesn't get to the other side, the police can pick it up and the owner can be identified! All police cars will have GPS systems that show little dots all the time of where the chickens are!"

"Wait … Chicken crosswalks! With lights in the shape of a chicken! That's it!"

"With little crossing buttons down low that they can peck to make the 'walk' light go on!" Nina and Maria were holding their sides now.

Chuck poked his head out of his door to see what was going on. The women stopped, looked at Chuck, and burst out laughing again. Chuck decided to go back into his office and gently closed the door.

In the previous chapter, we introduced the idea of association between variables but kept our discussion to nominal and/or ordinal data. In this chapter, we talk about the same ideas for interval data.

Association, relationships, and causality with interval data

You might think that determining whether there is a relationship between events or incidences or other phenomena is easier with interval data than it is with ordinal or nominal data because interval data are more precise. They're all numbers, right? Well, the fact that we have lots of numbers with interval data can make seeing patterns easier in some cases, but if there are too many points, too many variables, and too much "noise" in the data (like background noise in old recordings), it can actually be much harder.

In the last chapter we reviewed a series of questions that would guide us through testing for relationships. Here is the list again, with the normal English-language version first, followed by the statistical analyst–language version in parentheses:

1. Is there a similar pattern in the two sets of data? (Is there an association between the variables?)

2. If so, how strong is it? (What is the strength of the association?)

3. Is there a relationship between the two variables? (Is one variable having an impact on another? Do you think there may be causality?)

4. If so, what kind of relationship? (What is the direction and nature of that relationship? Which is the dependent and which is the independent variable?)

5. If so, is it statistically significant? (Is that relationship statistically significant?)

6. If so, does it really matter? (Is that relationship materially significant?)

Let's start with the idea of association with interval data. As with ordinal or nominal data, association is simply co-movement between two variables. With association, there is no independent/dependent variable designation because we have not yet established a direction of influence between the variables. We don't know if *A* influences *B* or if *B* influences *A* or if they both influence each other. All we know is that the two variables behave in a similar way: they move together. They do not have to move in a one-for-one pattern (which would actually be a perfect association); however, to show association, if there is a change in one, there must be a change in the other.

The most common measure used for association in interval data is called the Pearson's correlation coefficient (*r*). The computer does the calculation for you, so I will just focus on how to interpret what the computer spits out. Judging the strength of the association is actually pretty easy. The closer the correlation coefficient is to 1, either negative or positive, the more perfect the association. That is, the more perfect the co-movement, the more similar the two data series behave. If the correlation coefficient is 0, there is no correlation, no similar behavior, no co-movement. Of course, it is not often that we think that there might be a correlation and we come up with a perfect negative or positive one, or an absolute 0. Usually we are in between. The closer you are to the value of 1 (negative or positive), the stronger the co-movement. The closer you are to 0, from either direction, the weaker the co-movement.

So what does the negative and positive aspect mean? Are −1 and +1 the same? No. The sign of the correlation coefficient represents the nature of the association—whether it is negative or positive. Luckily, with interval data, it is much easier to visually see a negative pattern or a positive pattern.

One of the best ways to understand your information is to plot the values on a scatter-plot graph, with one data series along the bottom (the horizontal, or *x* axis) and the other data series along the left side (the vertical, or *y* axis). Each point is plotted on the graph, and you can see if there is a pattern. If you remember from the last chapter, a positive relationship is one where the values of the two variables increase or decrease in the same direction together. As one goes up, the other goes up. The way that analysts best understand the association in the data is to fit a line to the data. That is, the computer (thank goodness!) is able to plot a line along the data points. The line minimizes the distance from each point as much as possible.

Figure 9–1 is an example of a simple graph showing a positive relationship. You will notice that the line fits the data relatively well: the points are clustered tightly around the line. An analyst would say that the line is a "good fit" to the data.

A negative relationship is one where the values of the two variables increase or decrease together in opposite directions. As one goes up, the other goes down. A negative relationship looks like the one in Figure 9–2. As with the one above, the line fits the data well.

Both of these graphs show data with a strong association. The data are close together, and the pattern going up or down is clear. Most scatter plots are not so

Figure 9-1   Positive relationship with interval data

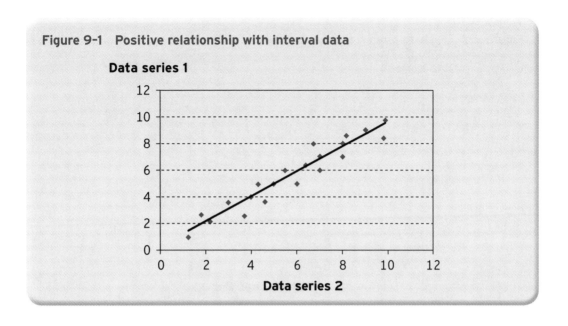

Figure 9-2   Negative relationship with interval data

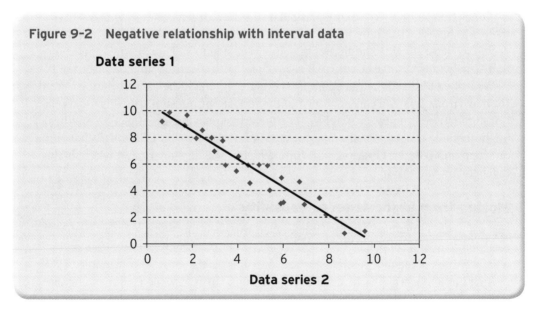

pretty. If the data are spread out but still generally go up in a pattern, the correlation coefficient will be positive but not as close to +1. Same thing if the pattern is loose but generally goes down: the coefficient will be negative but not that close to −1. The association, and accompanying correlation coefficient, will be weaker. What kind of association is reflected in Figure 9–3?

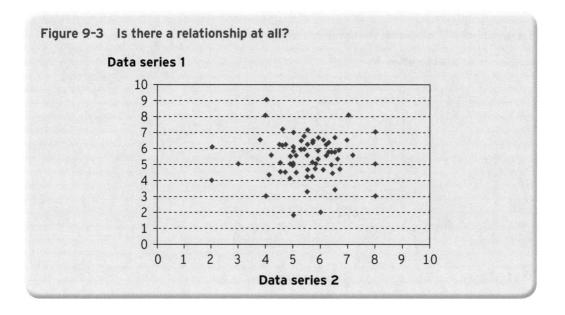

Figure 9-3   Is there a relationship at all?

None! No clear pattern in any particular direction. If you wanted to show that there was an association by fitting a line to the data, you would be hard pressed to decide whether the line should be up and down, side to side, or in any other direction. This would be an example of a scatter plot with a correlation coefficient of 0.

We have addressed the question of whether there might be an association, and if so, how strong it is. We can now turn to the rest of our questions: Is there is a relationship between the two variables? (Is one variable having an impact on another? Might there be causality?) And if so, what kind of relationship is there? (What is the direction and nature of that relationship? Which is the dependent and which is the independent variable?)

Moving from association to causality

Just like with nominal and ordinal data, when we reach this point, moving from association to relationship and then to relationship with causality, we need to identify what we think is the independent variable and what is the dependent variable. We are moving into the world of a **bivariable regression.** Which variable is influencing the other, in our opinion? Sometimes we ask, thinking in terms of our diagrams with arrows pointing from one variable to another, what is the direction of the relationship?

Approach causality with caution, however! Although we think of ourselves as pretty smart for a species, in the world of research, nothing can be absolutely proven. Remember how we discussed probability? There is always a probability that we are wrong in our conclusions, even if that probability is minute. Plus, when we set out to test for causality, we make assumptions about what is influencing what.

We guess in what direction the relationship runs. Does economic growth have an influence on education, or does education have an influence on economic growth? *We* have to pick the relationship we want to test.

Approach causality with caution!

Once we move into the world of causality and our scatter plot is not just two series of data but, rather, one series representing the independent variable (always on the *x* axis) and another representing the dependent variable (always on the *y* axis), we use the measure of association we just covered—the correlation coefficient—in our estimation for goodness of fit. But we don't just accept the value of *r*—no, that would be too easy! *R* represents goodness of fit for association purposes. Causality is a much bigger deal! We have higher standards! For causality, we use the measure called the r^2; it is just that, the correlation coefficient squared. But it is still a measure of goodness of fit.

To be technical, r^2 represents the amount of variance in *y* that can be explained by *x*. In more simple terms, you might think of it as how closely *y* is tied to *x*. In a perfect one-to-one match, if you know *x*, you would automatically know *y*. Turn that around: any differences between values of the dependent variable (variance in *y*) would be paralleled by differences in *x*.

Regression is about how much of your dependent variable (*y*) can be explained by the independent variable (*x*).

The huge difference in understanding patterns with interval data as opposed to nominal or ordinal data is that we can not only understand that there is a pattern but also describe the exact nature of that pattern! We can fit a line to our scatter plot of data, correct? We can follow that line and know that at any point for a value of the independent variable, or *x*, we can estimate the associated value of the dependent variable, or *y*. Once we fit a line to the data, we can get the equation for the line and know the exact nature of the relationship between the two variables! Think back to high school: do you remember the formula for a line?

$$y = mx + b,$$

in which *m* represents the slope of the line (rise over run, or change in *y* over change in *x*), and *b* represents the intercept of the line. We can use our interval data to plot the line.

Let me give you a simple example. On the night of the budget book preparation, when most of the budget staff have to stay late to get everything just right before the council budget retreat the next day, Chuck decides to order pizza for everyone. He gets the local pizzeria special, $5 for a single topping large. He orders 10 pizzas for the staff and looks at the final bill. It is $50. The total cost *depends* on the number of pizzas ordered. As Table 9–1 shows, there is a direct relationship between the number of pizzas ordered and the final bill. It is a positive relationship. As more pizzas are ordered, the total bill goes up.

Table 9-1   Pizzas and total bill

Number of pizzas	Total bill ($)
1	1
2	10
3	15
4	20
5	25

Plot the line yourself on a scrap of paper, with an *x* and *y* axis. In this example, what is the dependent variable? The total bill! Remember, it depends on the number of pizzas ordered, the independent variable. And what is the exact nature of the relationship? If we plotted the data, we would have a straight line. With a change in *x* (say, one more pizza ordered), there is a corresponding change in *y* of $5. The formula for this line would be

$$y = mx + by = 5x.$$

The slope is positive, so we know that the relationship is positive. As the number of pizzas goes up, the bill goes up. We interpret this by saying (in a deep, slow, academic, and potentially very boring voice), "For every one unit increase of *x*, the slope, also called the unstandardized beta coefficient, represents the corresponding change in *y*." *What?* In other words, for every pizza, the bill goes up $5.

But wait! The formula is missing something, isn't it? Where is the intercept? The intercept is where the line would start on the y axis and go up, in a perfectly positive, perfectly predictable way. Well, in this case, the intercept is zero, so we don't bother to even put it in. What would an intercept do in the example above? Well, what about the tip? Every good delivery guy or gal deserves a good tip, and of course, the local government offices want to keep up good relations with the local businesses, especially when the budget might include some new business fees. So Chuck always tips $10, regardless of how many pizzas are ordered. The formula for the line would become

$$y = 5x + 10.$$

In fact, we would say that we could explain all the variance in the bill (the dependent variable) every year Chuck orders pizza by knowing the number of pizzas ordered (the independent variable) and the tip (the intercept, or starting point). All the variance in the bill can be explained by the one independent variable: number of pizzas ordered—in this case, 10. So with all the variance explained, the r^2 is 100! I'll return to the value of r^2 in a bit, when we are discussing what the computer produces when we hit the "go" button for a regression analysis.

Alas, as we observed before, there are very few perfect relationships in the world. Usually, when we put data into a scatter plot, they don't fall into a straight line. It is more messy. The real world is always messier than abstract mathematics. How do we deal with that mess? By scooping it all up and dumping it into a term that we slap on the end of the equation: the **error term.** With the error term, our regression formula now looks like this:

$$y = mx + b + e.$$

Think about the lines that we fit to the data in the plots at the beginning of this chapter. None of the lines fits the data perfectly. There is always some error, some space left between the data points and the line. This is also why, in the real world, you are never able to perfectly explain all the variance in something. Why does the temperature go up and down? Why does it rain one day and not the next? Are weathermen and women ever really accurate? We know a lot about the atmosphere and geography and meteorology, but there is still some aspect of randomness in all science (and life). We can explain a lot but not all. So if r^2 is the amount of variation in the dependent variable that we can explain with the independent variable, we would hope for a high value of r^2 but not 100%.

The value of r^2 ranges from 0 to 1, representing 0% to 100%. In the first two figures in this chapter, the r^2 would be fairly high. But in Figure 9–3, the r^2 would be 0. One particular line would not be any closer to all the points than any other line. This might be the case of looking at the total pizza bill and plotting it against the hair color of the delivery person. There would be no relationship, no association, no causality between the two (I hope).

Multiple variable regression

Computers are amazing. Without computers, I can't imagine being able to move from the case of one independent variable to multiple independent variables. As I pointed out earlier, usually models include lots of factors, lots of independent variables. Think about economic growth in your community. Is it influenced by just one thing? Of course not. Economic development is influenced by population, climate, crime, employee skills, taxes, culture, incentives, interest rates, and on and on.

> Multiple variable regression lets us look at the big picture, all the variables at once, instead of one by one.

How can we look at the big picture, all at once? Are we limited to looking at possible relationships one by one? Luckily, no. To consider a second independent variable in a regression model, we simply add another x axis. Instead of seeing the scatter plot in two dimensions on a flat page, imagine a three-dimensional space, like the space in the room where you are sitting. Think of points floating in that space, as if you had a group of balloons floating in the room—some up high, some lower, some to one side, some to another. Imagine drawing a line through the room, through the balloons, so that the line is equally far away from each balloon. The line might cut low from one corner of the room to the upper corner on the other side. The line is drawn in such a way that from the direction of each *x* (along one wall or along the other wall), we can see the relationship between each *x* and the *y*, isolating each *x*, or each particular independent variable from the other independent variable. *We are controlling for the other independent variable, and just looking at the data one independent perspective at a time.*

All the interpretations we made for a bivariable regression are the same for a **multiple variable regression:**

- The r^2 is the same: it is the variation in the dependent variable, the *y*, that can be explained by all the independent variables (all the *x*'s) together.

- Each independent variable (each *x*) has its own slope, showing the impact that it has on the dependent variable. If that independent variable increases by 1, the value of the slope is the impact on, or change in, the dependent variable.

- There is still an intercept, showing the starting point (value) for the dependent variable.

- There is still an error term, which captures all the messiness that we can't explain through the independent variable that we have been able to include.

While regression is really valuable, it relies on some important assumptions in order for it to work well:

1. The model has to be well specified; that is, it should include all the variables that are important and no variables that are irrelevant. For example, to explain economic development, you would want to include variables on everything that influences economic development. That would be a lot of arrows on the page!

2. We assume that the model is linear—that we can fit a line to the data. Most analysts do not go beyond linear regression, but it is possible to fit a curve to data points, too. If you look at a scatter plot of your data and it looks like Figure 9–4, then head to the closest statistician's office and bring donuts. If you tried to fit a straight line to the data, you would get bad results. Remember the donuts. Fresh, hot glazed donuts if you are in a hurry.

3. We assume that there is no measurement error. Remember how, at the beginning of the book, we discussed validity and reliability in measures and in research design? This is where it is important. Just like with any of our analyses, garbage in, garbage out. If you looked at the extra garlic breadsticks that Chuck ordered and counted them as a $5.00 pizza even though they were only $3.50, your data would be wrong. This would not be good if you were a budget analyst for Chuck and he caught that error. He might start to wonder about your estimates for occupancy tax revenues.

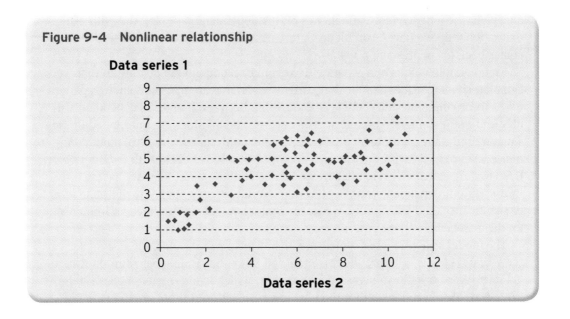

Figure 9-4   Nonlinear relationship

4. We also want to make sure that we measure things only once. For example, if you were measuring poverty in a community, you might use the variable average income. You might also want to use the variable of the number of children in the school who receive free or reduced price lunches. But these two things are really measuring the same thing—poverty—so if you include both of them in your model, the computer will not be able to appropriately assess the relationships involved.

5. Finally, we need to know that there is nothing funny going on in the error term: it truly represents only randomness, not hidden variables or patterns. There is a lot packed into this assumption, more than is going to be discussed here, and assessing the strength of this assumption can be difficult. If you go into the territory of multiple variable regression, I would recommend accepting this assumption with grace and crossed fingers or consulting a statistician.

You can see that with regression, more than with any other type of analysis in this book, we can get as close as possible to understanding the relationship between two variables. But we are left with two questions:

1. If so, is it statistically significant? (Is that relationship statistically significant?)

2. If so, does it really matter? (Is that relationship materially significant?)

Both of these questions can be answered with a focus on the regression coefficient, or slope, for each variable. For each variable, the computer has calculated a coefficient for us, correct? That coefficient is the estimated impact that one unit of change in the independent variable has on the dependent variable. And with estimates, what do we have? Confidence intervals and confidence levels! *YAHOO!* It all comes back to *t*-scores and *p* values.

Each variable will have a separate *t*-score and accompanying *p* value so that we can assess whether the data for that particular variable are in a tight enough pattern for us to be confident that there is a relationship between it and the dependent variable and not just a random pattern. The *t*-scores and *p* values are interpreted in the same way that they have been all along. Usually analysts use the breakpoint confidence level of 95%, with the associated *p* value of .05. Variables with *p* values below this level are statistically significant: we can be confident that they are having a real impact on our dependent variable. But other variables may not show the same level of significance, and we would have to conclude that they do not have an influence on the dependent variable.

The model as a whole has a measure of statistical significance, too. It is called the F-score. I know, I know, you are about fed up with the alphabet soup. But there is hope! It also has a *p* value associated with it, which is interpreted in exactly the same way. Just keep looking for the low, low *p* values, and those are the variables on which to focus.

It bears repeating: multiple variable regression allows us to understand both (1) the individual impacts that each independent variable has on the dependent variable (*y*) through the statistical significance measures (the *t*-scores and *p* values with each variable) and the unstandardized beta coefficients (the slopes, or material impacts), and (2) the statistical significance and explanatory power of the model as a whole (the *p* value associated with the model F-score and the model r^2).

There are many nuances to using and interpreting regression. I have not covered all the assumptions, all the various tests and numbers that would be on a printout, or when to choose this value over some other value when reporting results. Even if I did, you would not remember those rules when you were actually faced with data and an audience demanding help, such as a citizen group or the council or board. The explanation in this chapter is to help you understand that a sophisticated tool does exist that can not only say if there is a relationship between two things, like the number of pizzas and the bill, or tax breaks and economic growth, but also help us to understand the exact nature of that relationship.

Chuck put the phone down and was quiet for a little bit. He stood

up, opened the door to his office, and sat back down. It was after hours, and no one was in the office. He sometimes stayed late on Tuesdays, cleaning up things that the council had asked him to do. He hated to let those kinds of things sit for a couple days because you never knew what else would come up. And if nothing happened, well, there was the golf game and pizza to enjoy.

But would there be something like that in Scotts Bluff, which had just asked him to become one of the final four candidates for its manager? Would there be guys like Will and Rex? And what about Yvette? They had been on the library board together for a year, and he really enjoyed the meetings—and not because of the thrill of deciding on new shelving or how to raise money to refurbish the elevator. He realized he enjoyed seeing her each week. The last couple meetings they had even gotten coffee afterward to talk about books they liked and gossip about the retiring librarian.

Still, it was really appealing. Scotts Bluff was a much bigger city than Council Top, and it was a natural thing for a manager to be around for a couple years and then move on. At first he was really excited—the chance to be a manager in a place with a larger staff, larger budget! And larger issues, of course. Plus, it had done a lot for his ego. The recruiter said that the council in Scotts Bluff had heard about the advances in Council Top—steady growth, high citizen satisfaction, the ability to use information to defuse contentious issues, and good communication with the press and community groups.

Now he had to commit to participate in an assessment process. He would have to be public about the search and the chance that he would leave. If he went for it but didn't get the job, he knew that he would have burned bridges and that his time in Council Top would be short, even if everything was civil and they were supportive. No one likes to be considered second best or a steppingstone.

If he did leave, he would suggest that Nina apply for his position. She had developed an excellent reputation with the council. Her position had been elevated to assistant manager for management and budget. The council members loved her. When she discussed an issue, she talked as if she knew all aspects of the issue and had given them equal consideration. Rather than jump to conclusions, she gathered information and questioned every assumption, even if it took some time. She was slow to draw conclusions, but when she made a recommendation, it was firm. And she had clearly been able to hire and bring on talented staff. Maria had been working full time as assistant manager for special projects for over a year, and the other former intern, Max, was filling in for a budget analyst who was out on family leave and not likely to return. He was as good as Nina and Maria had been, if not better.

The city would be in good hands.

Chuck flipped open his phone, and then stopped and closed it. He opened it once more and punched in a number.

"Hello, Yvette? This is Chuck. I've been meaning to ask you something for awhile. Would you like to go to a movie this weekend?"

Review questions

1. What is a measure of association?
2. How would you interpret a correlation coefficient of 0?
3. Why can't you use regression with the following variables?
   a. The influence of a person's sex on his or her hair color
   b. The influence of whether someone smokes and the kind of car she or he drives
4. A regression line is sometimes called the "best fit." What do you think this means?
5. What is a regression coefficient?
6. How would the regression equation for Table 9-1 change if you always gave the pizza delivery person a $5 tip?
7. What is the difference between a bivariable regression and a multiple variable regression?
8. What is measured by r^2?
9. If you performed a regression analysis, looking at the influence of temperature and rain on crop yields (e.g., how many bushels of corn are produced per acre), how would you interpret an r^2 value of .85?
10. A person's memory improves as he or she grows from a child to an adult, but then it gets worse again with age. Could linear regression be used with this example to show the relationship between age and memory? Explain why or why not.